ESCAPING THE
PINK COLLAR GHETTO

ESCAPING THE PINK COLLAR GHETTO

HOW WOMEN CAN ADVANCE IN BUSINESS

ROBERTA CAVA

KEY PORTER BOOKS

Canadian Cataloguing in Publication Data

Cava, Roberta
   Escaping the pink-collar ghetto

ISBN 1-55013-075-7

1. Women executives. 2. Women in business.
3. Vocational guidance for women.   I. Title.

HD6054.3.C38 1988   658.4'09'024'042

C88-094091-3

Key Porter Books Limited
70 The Esplanade
Toronto, Ontario
Canada M5E 1R2

Printed and Bound in Canada

88 89 90 91 92   6 5 4 3 2 1

CONTENTS

DEDICATED TO MY FATHER, ROBERT (BOB) HALLIDAY HASTIE,
WHO WAS PROMISED THE FIRST COPY OF THIS BOOK,
BUT PASSED AWAY ON APRIL 6, 1987.
HIS GUIDANCE AND CONSTANT LOVING SUPPORT WERE
INSTRUMENTAL IN MY SUCCESS.

INTRODUCTION

In May 1984, I began doing research for a seminar to be called "Escaping the 'Pink-Collar' Ghetto." A year later, in July 1985, I began writing this book.

The book is intended for women who are frustrated in their attempts to climb the corporate ladder or who have hit a dead end in a pink-collar job. (A "pink-collar" job is any office-support position with low pay and few company benefits.) My hope is that both seminar and book will confirm the achievements of women who have successfully transcended their pink-collar jobs and help women who feel trapped in such jobs to use their abilities more effectively to get the kinds of jobs they want.

This book describes management's point of view and shows women many of the reasons why they're not promoted. Numerous women are playing a losing game in business because they're "playing basketball on a football field." They simply don't know the rules for effective participation, or the correct methods for climbing the corporate ladder.

During my research, I found many business women who had experienced the same feelings of frustration in the work world as I had. Unexpectedly, a number of men also called me to suggest I offer them a seminar on "Escaping the Blue-Collar Ghetto." They insisted that many men don't know the "rules" either. Others suggested I put on seminars to teach men ways of dealing with the "new woman" that would help them avoid offending her. They wanted to know the new rules as they relate to working with women managers. It appears that men too are confused by recent changes and want to do the right thing.

Participants who attended my seminar were very enthusiastic. A frequent comment was: "I just wish this seminar had been available to me fifteen years ago — I wouldn't have wasted so many years in a low-level position — I could have used my capabilities better."

CHAPTER ONE

ON THE HOME FRONT

Women are three times more likely than men to sacrifice their careers for the sake of marriage and child rearing. But young women can no longer count on being "taken care of" all their lives. Three out of four women either never marry or lose their husbands through death, divorce or separation.

Table 1:1 Women as a Percentage of Total Full-Time Employment 1960-1986			
	EMPLOYMENT		
Year	Women	Total	Women as % of Total
1960*	36,014	64,757	55.6
1965*	44,494	75,728	58.8
1970*	61,051	91,597	66.7
1975*	88,761	123,567	71.8
1981**	112,041	150,445	74.5
1984**	100,008	136,158	73.5
1986***	96,320	131,527	73.2

* Full-time employment, as of January 31st
** Full-time employment, as of April 1st
*** Full-time employment, as of October 31st
Source: Canadian Bankers' Association

Traditionally, women were the self-sacrificing nurturers in family life. However, in the last couple of decades this has changed, partly because of simple economics, partly because of the liberating effects of the women's movement. Many families simply can't survive financially with only one breadwinner. And, as Table 1:1 shows, fewer women are willing or able to confine their priorities to marriage and child rearing, and more women every day are pursuing careers.

It is estimated that by the year 2000, two out of every three women over the age of twenty will be in the labour force.

WHERE DO YOU FIT?

Each group of women, be it single women, single mothers, married women, divorced or widowed women, or women who are "empty nesters," has problems unique to it. If you're juggling family responsibilities with trying to get ahead in a career, the first thing you have to ask yourself is: "Will it be worth all the hard work and dedication I'll have to give to get there?" You must make a conscious decision and then act on it.

Being successful in a career is exhausting; it requires time, dedication, a good work ethic and "smarts." *But it can be done*!

If you have children and still want to give priority to your career, your first task is to obtain adequate care for them, so you can leave the worries of child care to others.

If you're single without dependents, or married with no children, I suggest you bypass the following information. If, however, you have a roommate or spouse who doesn't pitch in and help sufficiently, you might still find some of these pointers helpful.

FAMILY AS FIRST PRIORITY

If you have tiny children at home, you might have to say, "They deserve my full attention right now. They're my first priority, so I'm going to stay home with them." That's fine. But please don't just "mark time" while you're at home.

As I grew up, I assumed I would probably be like my mother and seldom, if ever, work outside my home. Therefore, when it came time for me to go to work, I had to play the game of catch-up. I should have realized the importance of using some of that valuable time as a full-time wife and mother to obtain competent career counselling and the education I would need. Then, when I returned to the work force, I would have been ready to step into a higher-level position than the one I had left. (As well, during the years at home with the children, I really needed to stretch my brain, to relieve the monotony of homemaking and child rearing.)

Even among those who choose family as their primary responsibility, many *have* to work for economic reasons. These women often need to lose their feelings of guilt for leaving their children. Psychological studies show children of working mothers develop as well as (sometimes better than) children with full-time mothers. It's how much a woman loves her children, how concerned and involved she is with them, and how happy she is with her life — not whether she works or stays home — that is important. However, there is often pressure on the working mother to accept a position of low responsibility, one that doesn't require the energy expected from management, but brings in a paycheque. If she decides to go this route, she'll have to stop feeling as if she's hitting her head against a wall trying to get ahead or promoted. She should leave that until later when her family responsibilities diminish. And she'll have to watch that "career women" don't make her feel as if her priorities are all wrong. The important thing here is that she makes the decision that's best for her — it shouldn't be made *for* her by others.

CAREER AS FIRST PRIORITY

If you go this route, you'll also have to prepare yourself mentally for the guilt feelings you'll have or that others will try to thrust upon you. If guilt is holding you back, this book may help you find the answer to turning it off or at least putting it on the back burner.

If you do decide your career is your primary goal, you'll also have to decide which family responsibilities should be delegated to others and obtain your spouse and children's reliable help and co-operation at home. If this help is not forthcoming, you'll probably have to hire someone.

Research tells us that when men with traditional views marry, most have no intention of changing the routine of their lives. They figure that, basically, they'll do the same things, think the same things, and be the same person, but as a married rather than a single man. In the past, women have often reshaped their personalities to conform to the wishes, needs and demands of their husbands, but this is now having to change in most households.

Do you have a traditionalist husband who still believes there should only be one breadwinner in the family? Has he "lost face" because it's now necessary for you to work? Is this the same husband that "helps" around the house by taking the garbage out once a week? If so, here's an approach that might help you obtain the necessary assistance.

If both of you have to work, you should bring certain facts to his attention. You're now sharing his traditional breadwinning role, so you need him to share the homemaking and child-rearing role. Don't ask him to "help you with . . ." He should be made to feel he's "helping himself with . . ."

The belief that the family unit is breaking down is becoming increasingly widespread, and the return of women to the work force is often cited as the cause of this breakdown. In families in which everyone works as a team this is just not so. Children who grow up to believe that Mom should make their beds and clear their dishes off the table, and that as children they're on this earth to have nothing but fun, are being deprived of one of life's important learning experiences. I believe you should never do for children what they can do for themselves. If you do, you only breed dependent, often demanding, children who expect a "free ride" through life, who depend on external things to make them happy, and who wait for others to provide them with what they want. These individuals never acquire the exhilarating feeling of independence that comes from knowing they can do whatever is necessary to succeed.

Don't underestimate a child's ability. Children become irresponsible only when parents fail to give them responsibility and the tools to fulfil obligations.

What if your family still won't help around the house? Try the following strategy for getting them to share the household responsibilities:

1. Write down *all* the chores that need doing around the house and yard. Include everything. Make a copy for each member old enough to read.
2. Call a family conference.
3. At the family conference, ask for all members to volunteer to do some of the chores. Fill in the chores you feel comfortable handling and have your spouse add his as well.

4. The remaining chores will then have to be assigned. (And don't let it be "dear old Mom" who takes them on; Mom doesn't have time either!) Even two-year-olds should have chores, such as:
   - picking up their toys;
   - putting their dirty clothes in the clothes hamper;
   - helping with the dusting, making shelves and drawers neat, or tidying shoes in a closet.
   Make sure your family knows you're counting on them to do the job right. Explain that you don't want to have to nag them to get their chores done and ask: "Can I count on you to do these chores?" Get a commitment from each of them. Then, like a supervisor, you must follow up and make sure they do the chores properly.
5. Give rewards. Signs of love and appreciation are necessary. Adults are normally rewarded for work well done; children should be too. You might put a monetary value on the chores the children are expected to do (in the form of an allowance) and deduct money for each breach of duty. Special family treats could be arranged for exceptional work.
6. Keep track of work completed. Make sure each child knows when duties are expected to be done. If they're constantly saying, "I don't have time," help them plan their time.
7. Make sure children have the training they need to fulfil their obligations.
8. Avoid power struggles. If children won't give you their word that they will do a task, ask them why. Acknowledge their reason and reply, "I know that taking out the garbage is not exactly a chore you like, but someone has to do it. Who do you think should be doing it?" Be willing to negotiate, but be firm and reasonable. If you are, the chore will usually get done.
9. For particularly unpleasant tasks, have a rotation system in which all family members capable of doing the chore take a turn.

If your family won't give a firm commitment to do the chores, you have two other choices. You can hire someone to help (which will reduce your family's overall income) and cut children's allowances, or you can quit your job (which will also reduce the family income).

If the man opts out of doing his share of home and child-care duties and you are still doing your share, the salary of the person hired should be paid by the husband. How do you think most husbands would react? If he objects, remind him of the principle of sharing breadwinner/homemaker responsibilities.

Parenting is a dual responsibility, and fathers should do their share in bringing up their children, plus their share in all the backbreaking work that goes along with keeping up a home. This is especially true if the wife works outside the house.

Women should have the opportunity to pursue a career if that's their desire. Husbands who object to this are being very selfish. If you feel you're slowly losing your sanity and the four walls are closing in on you, try this approach. Ask your husband if he would like to change roles for a while. You'll go out to work while he looks after the home and the kids. What do you think his reaction will be? The most likely answer would be, "I'd go nuts doing housework and being with the kids twenty-four hours a day!"

Your next comment could be: "Now you know how I feel. I'm going nuts doing housework and being with the kids twenty-four hours a day, and I need to work, the same as you do. If I work, I'll be happier, and so will everyone else!"

Another argument relates to income-tax brackets. The husband's objection goes as follows: "Are you crazy? We can't afford to do that! If we both work, it'll put me into another income-tax bracket."

Most income-tax specialists would agree that the extra income tax involved is more than compensated for by the income earned by the wife.

OVERCOMING OBJECTIONS

1. Your husband says that after your expenses are paid there won't be enough left out of your salary to make the "disruption" worthwhile. You can:
   - say that you *need* to work;
   - explain that you're going into a low-level position now, but that with training and education you hope to reach a higher salary level soon. Most people start at the bottom, and you can't expect to get to the top right away.

2. Your parents, your in-laws, and non-working female friends in the neighbourhood offer a variety of guilt-generating reasons why you shouldn't return to work or go back to school for upgrading. "Your kids need you, depend on you . . .," or, "Why did you have kids in the first place if all you wanted was to educate yourself and go back to work?" You should:
   - recognize they don't have the right to tell you what you should or shouldn't do with your life. *You and only you* can make that decision.
   - refuse to accept the guilt trips they're thrusting upon you. Your happiness spreads to your family. This is not a selfish wish. It is a necessity for your personal happiness.
3. Your husband would prefer you to get into volunteer work where you will be away only part-time. You should:
   - explain your need to do something that suits *your* needs, not his;
   - explain the benefits he and the children will have because you'll be happier.
4. Your husband says he is afraid that working all day will be too tiring for you. You should:
   - remind him that he has probably seen you get crankier and crankier, more and more tired around the home. He hasn't put two and two together to understand your crankiness and tiredness go hand in hand with your boredom. Explain this to him.
5. Your husband says it's okay for you to return to work, but you shouldn't expect him to help out much. He's too tired already when he comes home. You can:
   - hire someone to do his share of the housework and child rearing, to be paid for out of *his* salary.
6. Your husband says he already "helps" around the house. After all, doesn't he help clear the table after dinner and take out the garbage? You can:
   - explain that he isn't helping you — he's helping himself. It is *his* responsibility to do whatever is necessary around the house to get all the jobs done. This is not helping you, it's doing his share of the work.
7. You accept a position at the same level as his job. You're climbing fast, but he's hit a snag in promotional opportunities.

He's starting to show anxiety that you will overtake him and upset the balance of family power. This anxiety is revealed in a variety of ways. He may start belittling you and trying to sabotage your career by making you choose between your professional goals and his demands. Or he may stop "helping" around the home, withhold sex, become emotionally abusive or look to other women to boost his male ego. Initially you should:
- Try to discuss the problem openly with him. Ignoring it certainly won't help. As one of the more intractable problems of the two-career couple, this is probably worth a book of its own. You may need to seek professional counselling.

GIVING LOVING TIME TO YOUR FAMILY

Most women who work and are parents of young children face the following questions:
- When time is at a premium, how do I provide quality time with my children?
- How can I make sure my children get the love and attention they need when I'm away from home for more than eight hours a day?

Most women can't even ask their own mothers these questions because their mothers probably didn't have to face such problems. A conscious, planned effort must be made to provide this care without the guilt that often goes along with it. The following list is relevant to *both* parents.
- Spend individual time with each child that the child thinks of as his or her "special" time with the parent. This can be ten to fifteen minutes each day, or a set time on the weekend.
- Keep track of your children's "other lives" — at the baby-sitter, the day-care centre, kindergarten, school, sports and artistic activities, etc. Learn about special events at school and take time to attend. Encourage your children to keep you informed.
- Practise effective listening and try not to be judgmental. Don't make times with your children an inquisition. Hear what your children are *not* saying by watching their body language.
- Use effective time planning to eliminate unnecessary steps and tasks in order to give yourself more time with your family.

Establish your priorities, and remember to put your children high on the list of essentials.

- Enlist your children's help or ask for their presence when you're doing chores, so you can chat with them.
- Plan special outings that cater to individual needs. At a family conference, have each member state the special things he or she likes to do as a family. Try to utilize this list when planning special outings.
- Learn to be aware of your own stress level so you don't overreact to minor incidents with your children. If you've had a bad day, explain this to your children and ask if you can talk to them later. Don't put them off too long. Follow up on things they need to discuss with you.
- Don't feel guilty when you need "private time," and remember to honour your children's need for privacy too.
- Consider the following questions:
1. Do you feel you now provide quality time with your children?
2. Do you feel effective as a parent?
3. What immediate steps could you take to change 1 and 2?

If your answer is no to any of the above, I recommend Dr. Thomas Gordon's *Parent Effectiveness Training (P.E.T.)*. (Publication details of this and other books mentioned in the text are given in the bibliography.)

Your husband needs your "quality time" too. Try to plan some "wicked weekends" and holidays, so the two of you can rekindle the feelings of your early romantic days. Arrange often to go on "dates." Fuss and primp in preparation for these the way you did before your marriage.

EQUALITY
Consider the following story.

Two employees working for different companies are given the same assignment. One is a woman, the other a man. Each is married with a fourteen-year-old son and a nine-year-old daughter.

It's 2 p.m. An important meeting has been arranged for 9 a.m. in New York tomorrow. It's necessary for each employee to leave that evening on the 9 o'clock plane. There are no problems for the woman at work. Her problems occur at home.

MALE EMPLOYEE	FEMALE EMPLOYEE
Phones spouse, tells her about trip.	Phones spouse, tells him about trip.
At 6:15 wife serves *his* dinner.	At 6:15 eats dinner *she* has prepared.
Wife helps pack bag.	Packs own suitcase.
Wife checks list of items to be taken.	Checks own list of items to be taken.
Wife asks if he wants ride to airport.	Calls a cab so her husband won't have to go out of his way for her.

They return from their trips the next day at 8 p.m. Both are exhausted. Neither has eaten much since noon (their mouths are watering for a ham sandwich). They enter the front door.

MALE EMPLOYEE	FEMALE EMPLOYEE
Wife greets with kiss, asks about trip.	Husband is watching TV. Yells, "Hi, Hon!"
Kids yell, "Hi, Dad!"	Kids greet Mom describing what went wrong with their day.
He flops into chair in living room.	She flops into chair in living room.
He explains how tired he is.	She explains how tired she is.
Wife asks if he's eaten yet.	She asks, "Have you guys eaten yet?"
Wife makes him a ham sandwich and tea.	She starts to make herself tea and ham sandwich. Her son asks her to make him one, too (they had soup for dinner). Her daughter has one, too, and eventually her husband leaves the TV to ask for one. The ham runs out; she has tea and toast.
Wife unpacks *his* suitcase, finds a spilled bottle of aftershave lotion.	She unpacks *her* suitcase, finds a spilled bottle of hand cream.

Wife washes contents of his suitcase.	She washes contents of her suitcase.
Wife goes to bed, feels amorous towards him, but knows how tired he is. She covers him up and lets him sleep.	Husband goes to bed, feels amorous towards her, starts making advances. She mumbles, "I'm too tired tonight." She's shocked by his next comment: "I told you this job would be too much for you!"

An unshakable fact that many women fail to acknowledge is that men's lives are made a lot easier by the fact that they can come home to a caring, nurturing, empathetic partner. This partner is called a *wife*.

It's unfortunate that women don't have this luxury! If they did, half their frustrations and feelings that there's "something missing in their relationships" would be gone.

To learn more about this topic, I suggest you read *What Do Women Want? — Exploding the Myth of Dependency*, by Luise Eichenbaum and Susie Orbach.

Are you one of the lucky ones who has a "wife" at home? Many men are learning that nurturing doesn't have to be an exclusively feminine trait. It can be a very masculine characteristic as well. Men are learning how to nurture and how to be empathetic. When you come dragging in from work, such a man might say, "Had a tough day, Joan? How about a cup of tea?" Or, "Do you want half an hour to yourself while I fix dinner?" This is what a wife does, isn't it? Wouldn't it be great to have that luxury?

A man with these qualities usually had a mother who cared about him enough to teach him that he can show empathy and tenderness to those he loves and cares about without losing his masculinity. The man who doesn't have these qualities has probably been trained since childhood not to have them.

Carol Gilligan, a Harvard University psychologist and author of *In a Different Voice* (1982), observes that girls tend to be trained by their mothers to sense others' needs. They see themselves as part of a web of relationships and feel threatened by isolation. Meanwhile, many boys learn from their fathers to seek independent achievement. Ties to others threaten their self-esteem.

To most wives intimacy means sharing feelings. To most husbands it means sharing activities — going to a movie together, for example. When he's watching television, he wants her close by and wonders why she chooses to phone a friend. She can't understand why he's upset if she does this, when he's not even paying any attention to her.

Many wives find their female friends make better confidantes than their husbands. Quite often women live together because they provide "wifing" or nurturing for each other.

One of the things I find missing in my life right now is a "wife." In the past my son, Mike, gave me the kind of support many wives give their husbands. He was very good at it. It started when he was about fourteen and I was beginning to climb the corporate ladder, going to school in the evenings and handling a full-time job, as well as being a homemaker and a single parent.

I had called a family conference in which I explained that a lot of things had to be done in the next few years and that I was going to need all the help they could give me. My children learned to take a lot of responsibility and, as the older child, Mike took on more tasks than Michele. He made sure his sister (age seven) made it safely to school and back and cared for her till I got home from work. Initially, when he came home from school hungry, he would phone me at work to ask, "Mom, what do I do to get supper going? It's six-thirty by the time we eat, and I'm starving by then!"

He learned how to peel potatoes and progressed from there to making complete dinners for our family. Imagine how pleasant it was to come home to a hot, home-cooked meal every night! He's now living in another city, and I really miss his cheerfully given help. He'll certainly make some woman a good partner. He was also the "man around the house," and was able to do almost anything that needed doing. Together we finished one rumpus room, and he built another from scratch, on his own, two years later.

I encourage women to have this flexibility, too. They should be the "husband" at times and do some of the traditionally male jobs. They should carry the two-by-fours, use the paintbrush or roller, and try to do the kinds of chores husbands do. Women can do most of these tasks if they make the effort. Women can't expect men to change if they're unwilling to reciprocate.

Any shared chore is more fun. If you have a bedroom to paint, share the sanding and painting; if you work as a team, the job is done in half the time. It isn't just the man's job to paint. (Lorraine Giesbrecht, owner of a painting and decorating company in Edmonton, found business so brisk that her husband joined her when she couldn't handle all the potential work.)

Get a copy of Eichenbaum and Orbach's *What Do Women Want*, and give it to the men in your life. It's for husbands, lovers, fathers and sons. Before reading this book, few men really understand the meaning of the word "nurturing." Their mothers neglected to give them this essential training. Until recently, I didn't understand the empty feeling I'd often experienced in my life. I always had the impression that something was missing. Even when I was married or with a close male friend, there was always something lacking in the relationships. I could never put my finger on it. I didn't have a man in my life willing to nurture and help me the way I'd help him.

FEMINISM

One definition of a feminist is someone who is "very much for females — supportive of females." Another might be someone who believes in "women helping women." But to many people (both men and women) the term "feminist" conjures up the negative image of a bra-burning, radical, "far-out," possibly militant woman.

The latter description most clearly fits the majority's idea of a feminist. Women such as Betty Friedan and Germaine Greer, who were in the vanguard of modern feminism, brought the necessary attention to women's needs. They shocked the world by resisting inequality and challenging those in authority to accept women's equality. Their shock tactics worked, and women in the eighties have much to thank them for. They were the catalysts.

Feminism seeks equality for women in every facet of their lives. Feminists want the human "race" to end up as a "tie," not as a triumph of winners over losers. When someone calls you a feminist, be flattered. Reply, "Yes, I am a feminist because I believe in equality for both sexes." Be proud that you're among the growing number of women who are willing to be counted as favouring equality for all people. Most feminists working for equality today are low-key women who know how to negotiate, how to use psychology, and how to get a better deal for women. And their approach is working.

We often study a subject in school called "history," but now many women are in the process of making "herstory." News stories and articles about women who are making a name for themselves are becoming quite common. These women are our role models.

ATTITUDE

Most men are raised to believe that they'll have to support a family. Because promotions mean more money, they're willing to make sacrifices to reach the top. Instead of blaming others for not getting ahead, ask yourself whether it's because you lack the necessary drive and motivation.

CHAPTER TWO

WHY MANAGERS SAY THEY DON'T PROMOTE MANY WOMEN

As part of the research for this book, I asked managers to give me reasons why they weren't promoting women to management or decision-making positions. Many of their reasons are very valid, and women wishing to get ahead would be wise to listen to their explanations. These are things women have the ability to change, things that women are doing to hold *themselves* back. Women are often tempted to point to male chauvinism as the only reason for not being promoted, but as we'll see, only about twenty percent of the problem can be attributed to chauvinism (be it male or female). The other eighty percent is up to women.

BARRIERS TO PROMOTION

1. *Women haven't set concrete career goals for themselves.*
How can a manager help a woman get where she wants to go when she herself doesn't know where that is? This topic will be discussed in greater detail in Chapter 4.
2. *Women have problems working overtime and travelling on business when necessary. They're also unable to relocate when a promotional opportunity is available.*
This is a crucial one. Ask yourself the following questions:

Do *you* have any problems working overtime? If you do, what could you do about overcoming these problems?

Do you have any problems that keep you from travelling on business? Would your spouse object? Might a male travelling companion's wife object? What could you do about answering these objections?

Would you be able to relocate to another city if requested to do so by your company? What would your spouse think of this? What family problems would this cause?

These three related problems are at the top of the list of things that hold most women back from promotion. Why should your company expect male managers to work overtime at the drop of a hat, and not women managers? Why should just male managers have to travel on business? Why should your company only consider you for a promotion in the city in which you live? What makes you so special that these concessions have to be made for you?

You should discuss all three of these with your spouse so you know where you're at with him. You might be surprised at his answers, both for and against. These issues *have* to be resolved. You'll have to make sure your employer knows that overtime, travel and relocation are *not* problems for you. *Don't assume she or he knows this.*

3. *Women are often away because of their own or their children's illnesses.*

Employment records show that, on the average, women are off sick about the same amount of time as men. But they are absent more often than men on account of their children's illnesses. Ask yourself the following questions:

How much time do I take off work because of my children? In the last year, how many days have I had to take off because my children were sick or I had to take them to doctor or dentist's appointments?

Many mothers feel guilty if they don't take their children to doctors' appointments or stay home to look after them when they are sick. That's why it's so important to have good backup child care available. And it should be in-house help, because day-care will not accept a child with, say the measles. Grandma Moses down the street may not be suitable for full-time baby-sitting, but she may be ideal for such emergencies.

Have your backup person available to take your child to the doctor or dentist as well. Or find out if your doctor, dentist or health unit has weekend or evening hours. Always have somebody available to help out — your husband, your mother, or your aunt, but *do* have backup. If there's an emergency and the child is really ill, your employer will accept your absence much more readily if your child-related absenteeism has been infrequent. But, "Johnny's got a cold, so I'll stay home" is not likely to endear you to management when you're up for a promotion. They'd be justified in saying, "Uh-uh, forget it. She's away too often. She has a little kid at home, so she won't be here when we need her."

If, on the other hand, you're being held back from a promotion and your attendance is excellent, make sure they know about it by saying, "I was overlooked for a promotion, and I'd like to know why. It certainly isn't my attendance." But if you *are* away, you haven't a leg to stand on. They have the right *not* to promote you if your attendance is poor.

How much time do you take off work because of your own illnesses? I don't mean when you had to miss work because of surgery or a bout with pneumonia. That isn't the kind of absenteeism that bothers employers (unless it's chronic and long-term). I'm talking about casual illnesses involving absences of one or two days a month.

When you get into management, you're expected to be there! They rely on you. If you're absent too often, you're not going to be promoted. It costs the company too much money to pay you while you're away and not producing. Remember, the more you're earning, the more it costs your company when you're away.

Many employees assume that if their company gives them a day and a quarter a month paid sick leave, they should take it.

They think this is a right they have as employees. Wrong — it's a privilege that's given to you, and unless you need it, you're not expected to use it! Otherwise, you're taken to be a nine-to-fiver, and no promotional opportunities will be given to you. You're not a "company" employee — you're looking after "you and only you," and companies don't like it.

If you're getting into management, have "female problems," and are away one or two days a month — don't *ever* give that as your excuse for being away! If you have chronic problems in this area, go to a doctor and get treatment. If management sees you taking a day or so every month for your "female complaints," they're likely to decide they can't promote you.

Another serious problem that too many women don't recognize is premenstrual tension. I suffered terribly from this for approximately ten years before I understood what was happening to me. Doctors at that time treated my mood swings with Valium, almost as if I had a brain dysfunction rather than a hormone imbalance. However, when I realized what was causing the problem, I learned to handle it.

If this could be a problem for you, consult a doctor *and* try to find ways of mitigating any bad effects on your career. At this time of the month don't overburden yourself with tasks at work or at home that might put extra stress on you. Learn to plan ahead.

Don't give men in the office the chance to say things like, "It's her time of the month again!" Take care of your female problems.

4. *Women don't know their limitations and attempt to be Super-woman, Supermanager and Supermom.*

Even if you do not have children, or your children are grown, you should read this section. It will help you empathize with women who do have this problem.

Managers know that unless you have competent care at home, you're working at two full-time jobs. They know you can only do this for so long before you burn out, because they've seen it happen to their own wives or family members.

Does this fit your situation? Are you trying to fill three slots at once? Don't drag yourself to work in the morning and drag out at night. Trying to be superhuman is the biggest failing of women who're pursuing a career. They try *so* hard to be perfect at everything that there's nothing left for just "living" and enjoying what their toil has brought them. It's a good idea to let management know you have competent help at home and that you're capable of handling not only your existing position but other more complicated positions as well.

5. *Women bring their family and personal problems to work and waste time discussing them and worrying about them.*

How much time do you spend discussing personal matters at work? For example, "Patti graduated this weekend. Did she ever have a nice time . . ."; or, "We had a terrific weekend. We . . ." How do you rate? Is this one of your failings?

Managers are watching you — and what do they see? They see dollar signs. And these dollar signs are flying out the window because you are wasting not only your own time but that of the person you're talking to. Suppose you and your co-worker are earning ten dollars an hour; if the two of you spend just fifteen minutes per day in idle chat, you've cost the company five dollars. Multiply that by 200 working days, and you'll see that you're wasting about $1,000 of the company's money a year! That's what managers see. If you intend to get promoted, don't talk about anything except work-related matters during business hours.

If you must talk about something that happened on the weekend, do it at coffee or lunch break.

How many personal phone calls do you make a day? If your children "check in" with you when they arrive home from school, fine, as long as it isn't a long conversation. But beware of getting involved in domestic battles between two siblings who call you to be their referee.

Learn to compartmentalize your life. Turn a mental switch off when you leave home. If your children are properly cared for, you should be able to turn their problems off. If you had an argument with your spouse, turn that off, too. Concentrate on matters related to your job. Do the same thing when you come home — turn the work switch off. You must make a conscious effort to learn how to do this. It's deadly to be preoccupied, whether at home or at work. For instance, if you have taken a work problem home and little Margie is talking to you about something of importance to her, she knows when you're not really listening to her. You have to concentrate on giving quality time at both places.

6. *Women gossip.*

It's been said that people who gossip usually end up in their own mouth traps. I have to admit this is a bad habit with many women, especially those who don't wish to get promoted in business.

For women who're trying to get ahead, gossiping on the job is an absolute no-no. "What about the men who gossip?" you may ask. Chances are they aren't in management either. Don't participate in this destructive habit. How do you do this? For example, you hear that Millie's husband is charged with drunk driving: "Let's talk to Millie about it."

7. *Women don't stand up for their ideas and are afraid of confrontation.*

Women have traditionally been the peacemakers in history and have considerable trouble relinquishing this assumed responsibility. Men are familiar with confrontation and find it stimulating to have a lengthy debate. Unfortunately, women feel uncomfortable and aggressive when they're forced to defend their ideas. They back off. A common reason why women fail at confrontation is that they neglect to take enough time to prepare so that they can back up their positions with facts rather than emotions. These facts must not be assumptions and/or guesswork.

8. *Women with low self-esteem and self-confidence are afraid to take risks and try new things.*

We'll be discussing this issue in great detail in Chapter 10.

9. *Women are poor communicators and are misunderstood too often.*

I don't agree with management on this one. Women are far better communicators than most of their male counterparts. They communicate on a plane far above the level of most men, mainly because they use more communication methods. But men can be confused by women who use these extra methods.

Think of the young mother with a child still learning to talk. She uses two distinct communication skills that she hones to perfection — empathy (she puts herself in the place of the child), and her ability to read the child's body language. Some men are making an honest effort to acquire these skills (perhaps because they're accepting more responsibility in caring for their children). When they bring these skills into the workplace, everyone benefits.

10. *If their ideas are shot down, women react as though THEY are failures.*

A woman gives a suggestion to her boss, but it's rejected. The woman feels hurt, so instead of coming back with another suggestion that *will* work, she stops giving suggestions. Remember, the boss is rejecting *your idea*, not *you!* That's not what was intended by the rejection of the idea. Men take rejection of an idea as part of the "game." Women, unfortunately, take this kind of rejection personally. If they have an idea and it's turned down, their response is "Nobody's going to listen to me — so why bother?" It's a form of rejection they practise on themselves.

What do you think you should do if your idea has been shot down? You betcha!! Get back in there, and come up with a second and possibly a third suggestion. If you don't, you'll be thought of as a "sissy" (a most derogatory term when aimed at men) because you gave up. If you make a good suggestion to your boss, and she or he says, "No, I don't think that will work," it doesn't mean you should never come up with another idea. You may revise your original suggestion, but you keep on plugging.

I've learned to have Plan B on the back burner, and often Plan C as well, in case I need them. These extra plans are developed by brainstorming and coming up with as many solutions as possible. I then take the best solution and try it out. I have the others as backups if the first one doesn't work. Or I may have to look at the whole problem in a different light and rethink it completely.

11. *Women have indirect ways of getting what they want — "female tricks" such as crying, pouting, having temper tantrums, acting "cute" or acting seductive.*

These are manipulative ploys that women have been conditioned to believe will work. But such devices don't work. Moreover, as far as I'm concerned, women put themselves down when they use these tactics. Be "up front" when you want something. Learn to ask for things directly instead of playing manipulative games.

Bosses frown on women's tears in the workplace. It used to be thought that if a female broke down and bawled it was "the way women are," which provided an excellent excuse for keeping them out of the executive offices. The rules in business say that you simply don't cry. Men don't know how to deal with it. (Unfortunately, women cry four times more often than men.) Most women executives are never seen crying. They have become tough enough emotionally to save their tears for somewhere other than the workplace — even if it's only the women's washroom. Men are more likely to show their emotions through aggression. They'll yell, kick the garbage can or punch the wall — but they won't cry! This reaction is just as bad (or worse) than crying, but seems to be tolerated by men in the workplace.

Women who act cute or wear frilly "little-girl" outfits, or use the "poor helpless me" approach make all women look bad. Most people are turned off by these tactics.

The same goes for people — men and women — who resort to tantrums to get their way. People who have tantrums on a regular basis are immature and insecure, and management will take note. Most adults can control their reactions, but some never learn this control. People who have temper tantrums have learned that if they kick up enough fuss, they'll get their way. They've been using these tactics since they were children. My children each had *one* tantrum — *one*. Then they realized it just wasn't going to work for them.

Tantrums often happen when these people are tired or have run into what they see as insurmountable obstacles. No matter what the reason, these tactics are not only childish but very disruptive in an office setting. These people don't appear to realize they're alienating others.

Wearing low-cut, seductive outfits and "acting sexy" also net only the most limited of short-term gains. If you do this, people will assume you got where you are not by merit but by granting sexual favours. It may get you a few rungs higher up the ladder, but only a few.

Businesses are looking for professionalism, and there's nothing professional about that kind of dress or behaviour. Ask yourself if you want people to see you as a businesswoman or as a female.

How to dress for business will be covered in Chapter 10.

12. *Women sabotage other women when they're promoted.*
Some women sabotage other women when they've been promoted into a position of power or into ranks dominated by men. This will be discussed in Chapter 8.

13. *Women are unable to make independent decisions when necessary.*
Some women stay clear of making decisions and expect others to make them for them. If you haven't read *The Cinderella Complex* by Colette Dowling, do so soon. Dowling discusses why women are often dependent on others to make their decisions for them, and how this early social conditioning can be overcome. Women have to learn that it's okay to make their own decisions, that it's their right, and that it's necessary if they are to succeed in business.

Traditionally, women are taught from childhood to rely first on their parents and then on their husbands for confirmation of every decision they make. They have learned to feel inadequate and incapable of making correct decisions. Most women feel they must get the advice of at least one other person before they make a decision.

Ask yourself, "When I have a major decision to make, either at work or in my private life, how many people do I consult before actually making the decision?" I can almost guarantee you'll consult at least one other person, whether it's a girlfriend, a husband, a boss or a co-worker. You probably feel you have to get someone else's approval before taking that decision-making step. Certainly get information from others upon which to base the decision, but don't be afraid to make that decision. Use your intuition. If it feels right, run with it.

Dowling explains that she was very capable of making decisions as long as there were no males around. As soon as a man was around she forfeited that decision-making right to the fellow she was with. When I read the book, I had just broken up with a man, and that's exactly what I had done as well — forfeited all my decision-making powers to him. It hit me like a bolt of lightning, how similar I was to her. I too had been making decisions for myself and my children since my divorce without consulting anyone; but as soon as a man came into my life that I thought I might spend my life with, I turned over that right to him. I doubt that he wanted it.

The first major decision I made in my life was to get divorced, and thereafter decisions were made daily. Was that hard to do! I encourage all women to live on their own before they marry. This ensures that they'll learn how to make independent decisions. Otherwise, they're going from one dependent situation to another, without "trying their wings."

Dependent women expect others to look after them. They wait for something external to change their lives. Setting goals for themselves is out of the question, unless someone else advises them and helps them do it. These women seldom have to make decisions until their spouse dies or they become divorced. Even when they're on their own, they find themselves looking for someone who can make their decisions for them. When they remarry, they relinquish decision making again.

This conditioning of women to rely on others is often brought into the business world. It's common for women to procrastinate, using a variety of excuses to avoid the responsibility of making a decision. Managers are right when they say that few women are able to make decisions without involving others.

We've discussed the reasons managers gave for not promoting women. Here are some ways in which managers thought they themselves might be holding women back.

1. *Some male managers often overlook women for promotion out of protectiveness.*

Because men are taught traditionally that it's their duty to be the decision makers, many feel very uncomfortable having a woman in a decision-making position. Others don't consider women for promotions because they want to protect them from the demands of management responsibilities. This is not done to put women down, but because they feel women need to be sheltered from "the jungle out there."

2. *Some male managers overtrain women before they set them free to use their training.*

Managers seem to think that a woman needs twice as much on-the-job training as a man before she's ready to step into the next position. But if managers looked more closely, they'd see that many women train the person who ultimately gets the promotion. This happens over and over again: a junior man starts with the company, is trained by a senior secretary (possibly you), and then starts on his way up the ladder to management.

Your bosses, by the way, love having you where you are. You provide them with the best training resource of all, and you're inexpensive to boot! Without you they would have to pay a fortune for that kind of on-the-job training! Know your worth. Your employer would be foolish to promote you under these conditions. You've got to take steps to stop this from happening in the future.

Women in this situation should explain their position to their bosses by saying, "This isn't right! I've trained Harry — I've trained Joe — and I've trained Bill. If I was capable of training them, why am I being overlooked for a promotion? I'm capable of climbing that ladder myself." Listen to what your boss has to say. It's up to you to let your boss know that you don't like being overlooked (you'll keep getting overlooked as long as you remain silent). Stand up for what you feel is right and fair — but by using facts, not emotions. Ask your boss to put your name down for the next promotion and to give you the opportunity of applying for it. Explain *why* you think you deserve the promotion. You might also ask your boss what's missing in your background that would improve your chances.

3. *Some managers promote women into positions for which they have had little or no training.*

For instance, more women than men are thrown into supervisor's positions without supervisory training. Many are initially going to be clerical supervisors, so management assumes training isn't necessary. But *any* supervisory job requires training if it is to be done properly. If you need it, get it!

4. *Some managers fail to provide up-to-date job descriptions.*
Many positions lack job descriptions, so the employee wanders
around trying to discover what she's expected to do. She's forced
to re-invent the wheel. That's tough on the employee, especially if
her predecessor left before the position was filled.

You often hear new employees say, "Oh, was I supposed to do
that?" Even their bosses may not know all the duties of the job
because they may not have worked closely with the former
employee.

If you're placed in a position of not knowing what you're to do,
ask your boss for a written job description. You need to know what
your priorities are and what your boss wants from you. How can
your boss possibly evaluate how well you do on the job if neither
of you knows what you're supposed to do? Every position you
work in should have an accurate, up-to-date job description. Many
companies will give the excuse, "Well, we don't have job descriptions in this company." Offer to write your own; then have your
boss go through it with you so you'll both know what's expected of
you.

5. *Women are discouraged from imitating men in business and told to
use their "unique" talents and abilities instead.*
Many top management people state that women *can* act differently from men in business. This is false. It's a fact that, right
now, if women don't follow the unwritten rules of business, they'll
fail. Many men don't like the rules either, but they abide by them
as if they were written down. Perhaps when more women reach
top management, the games that are played will become obsolete.
In the meantime, though, women should learn to play the game
within the existing rules, no matter how goofy and insane some of
them appear. This will be covered in Chapter 3.

6. *Most men stay clear of any woman they perceive as a "women's
libber." Aggressiveness in men is still tolerated but is absolutely
forbidden in women.*
Oh how true this is! Men and women have been putting up with
aggressive male bosses for centuries. Are these bosses liked?
Hardly — but they *are* obeyed. Now the female boss enters and
tries to copy the behaviour of the aggressive male boss. She's
immediately disciplined and/or demoted. This tactic simply
doesn't work for women and soon won't for male managers either.
This topic will be covered in Chapter 10.

CHAPTER THREE

GAMES PLAYED IN BUSINESS

It's been said that there are two ways to climb the corporate ladder — by climbing over other people, or by developing your subordinates and letting them push *you* up. Obviously, the second route is the most effective.

Unfortunately, most women don't get the chance to climb over anyone because they seldom get the chance to put their feet on the first rung of the corporate ladder. Many of them have spent their lives working in a support role and don't know how to get out of that role into upper management. No matter how hard they work or how dedicated they are, or how sincere their wishes for promotion — somehow they're consistently passed over.

This happens because most women don't realize business is a game — the game of Corporate Politics. All profit-making companies follow the rules of this game. Here is an example of what I'm talking about.

The most crucial rule is that businesses are out to earn money — not spend it! Everyone is expected to be dollar conscious. If you can think of something that will save your company money, you'll be listened to, provided you've got the facts to back it up — and provided you present the idea in a way the people in charge can relate to.

If you have an idea of this type, don't go on and on about how much easier it will make Tom's job. Instead, try to put a dollar value on how much money your company will save if your idea is adopted. For example, "This will save our input workers time and therefore save the company X dollars per unit." A couple of extra tips: remember, if your idea is not accepted right away, don't give up; and don't use such phrases as: "I feel . . . I think . . . I believe it will work."

The rules sound simple — obvious even. But because they are *unwritten*, it can take a lot of time to figure out what they are.

Most women who've stepped over the support-staff boundary into the executive game are completely unaware that on the other side of the barricade is a foreign country with customs, conditions, unwritten rules and ways of its own. The new female manager who doesn't realize that the natives in this new world speak a different language may wonder at first why she feels disoriented. Then she will wonder how she can learn what she needs to know as quickly as possible, only to come up against another problem. Not only are there no road maps in business, there are no written rules of the game (at least not any that women can see), but men seem to feel it's instinctive when they act and react as they do in business. So if you ask them to explain what's happening or why they did what they did, they probably can't tell you what triggered their action, except that it felt right.

What do men know that women don't? How can rules be adhered to by men, you say, if they're not written down? They've been taught these rules, bit by bit, through participation in competitive sports, through time spent in military services, and through time spent working with, talking to, and observing other men who know the ropes.

Although most women feel that games are childish and that business should be conducted in a straightforward manner, they have to understand that because these rules are rigidly adhered to by *successful* men and women, they'll have to conform (at least as things stand now).

You may not like these rules personally, but at least now you'll know when you're breaking one.

I broke a lot of rules — and didn't know I was breaking them. I felt very frustrated because I didn't know what I'd done wrong.

If you decide you just can't hack the kind of game playing that goes on in business, you might decide to opt out, and start your own company. Entrepreneurs are discussed in Chapter 14.

GAME PLAYING IN BUSINESS

If you haven't read Betty Lehan Harragan's *Games Mother Never Taught You — Corporate Gamesmanship for Women,* you should do so immediately. It will open your eyes to what is really going on in business. For example, she explains that working is a game women never learned to play, that having women players on the team upsets the "boys," and that it's important for women to learn to take charge, replacing passivity with the habit of command.

When I finished reading Harragan's book, I felt very angry. I was not angry at her for identifying these games; I was angry that no one had ever explained them to me and that I had been oblivious to them. I suddenly realized why I had handled so many things incorrectly in the past; all the frustrations, barricades, double-dealing, backbiting and buck passing I had been subjected to in my climb up the ladder now made sense. I had always felt I was "out of synch" with the business world, and I realized many women felt the same way. I vowed to keep as many women as possible from making the same mistakes I had. By applying some of Harragan's insights to my own experience, I came up with the following sixteen rules.

RULE 1: NEVER UNDERMINE YOUR IMMEDIATE BOSS BY GOING OVER HIS OR HER HEAD TO THE NEXT LEVEL.

I committed this *faux pas* over and over again, and I just wasn't allowed to get away with it! After I understood that the hierarchies of business reflect the sort of chain of command you find in the military, I knew better.

All the rules in business are based on a combination of military regulations and the rules of competitive sports.

In sports, men learn that if their coach tells them to do something, they'd better do it! And if their boss tells them to do something, they also do it. We have to learn to do the same. If you go above your boss's head to her boss and say, "I don't like the way she's supervising me," her boss isn't likely to do anything. His or her attitude will be, "I pay your supervisor to do her job, so listen to her and do what she says!"

Every task you do makes your boss look either good or bad, depending on how you complete the task. If your boss tells you to do something, do it his or her way (within reason of course), not your way. Once you understand that ultimately *they're* as responsible for your tasks being completed properly as you are, you'll understand why you should do it "their way."

The ultimate person in importance to you is your immediate supervisor *who has the power to promote you, demote you, or fire you.* Nobody else! Your supervisor's boss won't step in on your behalf; that's just not supposed to be done in business. I'll bet you weren't aware of this. I can't tell you how many times I went over my boss's head (especially if I thought he was incompetent), trying to get someone, anyone, to "listen to some sense." It didn't seem possible to me that businesses would let someone be in a position of power with so little knowledge. I felt it was my obligation to pass on my brilliant ideas to my boss's boss, if my boss wouldn't listen to them. Wrong, wrong, wrong! His boss didn't dare listen to me, or he'd undermine the whole system!

Recruits in the military learn that their senior officer is entitled to their respect and unquestioned obedience. This deference is given *solely* on the grounds of rank. This means no matter how incompetent the person is, you're still expected to show respect! I couldn't and still can't understand this tradition. If my boss was incompetent, I found it impossible to work for him or her. You may shake your head and say, "I can't handle that rule either." That's unfortunate, because you'll have to abide by it. No more going over your boss's head! You may gain a small victory by identifying your boss's weaknesses, but in the long run you've just set yourself up to fail.

Suppose you find yourself reporting to this kind of boss. You're having a difficult time working for him or her, and you feel like going over his or her head all the time. You have three choices:
1. Put up with the situation as long as you can (possibly until you're ready for the next promotional level).
2. Make a lateral move to another department.
3. Get out as quickly as you can (move to another company).

If you decide to take a lateral move to another department, the position will most likely be in another specialty area. Suppose you want to stay in your original specialty area? You can get back to it by doing the following:

Work towards a promotion in your new department (which will

make you a peer of your former boss); then, when an opportunity arises for you to apply for a promotion in your original specialty (making you your former boss's boss), apply for it. Now guess who has control? Your former boss is not likely to get there before you, if she or he is as poor a manager as you believe.

Remember, it's the position that matters, not the person in it. You're hired to fill a position; the position is not set up to meet your needs. The job is not going to adapt itself to you or your abilities. You're out of luck unless you have the advantage of working for one of the few progressive companies that are adapting or starting new positions to take advantage of the unique talents and abilities of employees. These firms are few and far between.

RULE 2: DO ONLY YOUR JOB AND ITS DUTIES — NO ONE ELSE'S.

Normally, if companies hire you to do a job, they expect you to do that job and nothing else. Catch yourself if you're slipping over into someone else's area of responsibility.

"Don't help me when I don't ask you to help me!" is sometimes the comment of male peers when women make this blunder. Most women who've worked at home for a few years come back into the work force with the same attitude to work that they had at home. If they saw a job that needed doing, they simply rolled up their sleeves and did it. That won't work in the business world. Do your job and no one else's, no matter how much you're tempted to pitch in. When all your work is done (and only then), *offer* to help another worker. But finish *your* work first.

Denise's job was to process reports. She found she spent half her time correcting mistakes she found on the documents. What should Denise have done with those reports? She should have sent them back to the person who made the mistakes. Whose job was she doing? That of the person who prepared the reports. Who looked good because the reports were correct? The person who prepared the reports, not Denise. Who looked bad because she wasn't getting her own work done? Denise. She explained that she didn't want the other person to look bad, so she helped her out. If the errors had been minor, requiring only small corrections, of course she should have made them, but she shouldn't have been spending her valuable time correcting someone else's major blunders. As well, if she had made changes that turned out to be wrong, she would have been at fault.

RULE 3: DEMONSTRATE RESPECT — AND AVOID SHOWING DISRESPECT — FOR YOUR BOSS.

Politicking, apple polishing, brown nosing and bootlicking; they're all the same thing. To many women this is phony baloney in spades, and they refuse to take part in it. You see a male colleague outside his boss's office preening before he goes in. You see him showing respect, even deference to his superior. You can't understand why the colleague puts on the show when you know he hates his boss with a passion, believes he's an absolute idiot, and certainly doesn't respect him.

I agree, it's not honest. And I can't do it. But in business, believe me, you're expected to do exactly that. You're expected to show respect to your boss whether or not you think she or he deserves it. That's tough for most people to do.

Other things that *could* be considered bootlicking are:
- having the boss and his or her spouse over for dinner, or taking them out for dinner;
- currying favour by giving senior staff free tickets to sporting activities;
- doing anything underhanded to make you look good in the eyes of your boss.

Many people look for their boss's "hot button" and push it. They spend time analysing what they can do to get on his or her right side. This has nothing to do with doing a good job; it's far more manipulative than that. If I were a boss and saw this going on, my respect for the person using these tactics would diminish . They certainly would not get any "Brownie Points" from me.

Male subordinates may take their boss out for dinner. Females are more likely to say, "Hey, my private time's my own." These women opt out of this aspect of the game. They might do good work while refusing to maintain a deferential, respectful manner. Women are more honest about this, and it causes a lot of waves in business.

If you really want to succeed, you're at least going to have to pretend to like your boss. You may decide to opt out of this game, but when you break this rule, you'll now know you're breaking it.

RULE 4: BE WARY OF ACCEPTING A PROMOTION THAT HAS ALREADY BEEN TURNED DOWN BY A MAN.

You might initially say, "Great — I've been offered a promotion!" You should stop and ask yourself why George didn't take it when it was offered to him. I suggest you talk to George and find out why *he* didn't take it. You might find there's something really wrong with the position. Maybe that job is going to be obsolete in six months' time, or perhaps the boss you would report to is impossible to work for. George knows something you don't — so you owe it to yourself to ask him about it before accepting the position.

Have you ever taken a position where you had been set up to fail and didn't even know it?

If you're offered any job and have reservations about it, ask for more time to make your decision. Then investigate. In the above example, it's possible George had his eye on another job and your worries were unfounded — but do check it out.

RULE 5: DON'T ACCEPT MORE AND MORE RESPONSIBILITIES. KNOW YOUR LIMITS!

This one is a major failing of women. Some men fall into this trap, but it's mainly women who do it. Picture a woman at a desk with mounds and mounds of work on it and more and more coming in. She keeps going at top speed, but no matter how hard she works she never gets to the bottom of that pile. How frustrating that must be for her!

One thing she might do is take a course on time management to learn how to set priorities in her work. In time-management courses, she'll be taught how to identify the rush jobs that have to be done right away, the jobs that have to be done today, and those that can be put off until tomorrow. The first ones she tackles, of course, are the rush jobs. They're all looked at, and she decides which one has top priority, second priority, third priority, etc. The other two groups of tasks she puts into folders or baskets, preferably in another part of her work station. Then she determines how much time it will take to complete the tasks that need to be done that day. If she realizes at this point that she can't handle all the tasks, it's time to speak to her boss and ask his or her opinion.

Because she's now on top of what she can do that day, she'll know what to say when extra tasks are dumped on her desk. She'll be able to say, "I'd be happy to do that, but I don't have time." Or, "Does this take precedence over the rush job you gave me before lunch?" This leaves the decision up to the person giving her the work. Or she could say, "I'm sure you want this task professionally done, but if I'm going to do both assignments in that space of time, I don't think it'll have the quality you want. Do they both still have to be done by noon?" The supervisor then makes the choice, not her. This will make her boss realize she's organized enough to know when she's in over her head. It makes her look very professional.

Some superiors keep giving more and more tasks until the employee complains and asks for a raise. Then the supervisor explains his or her displeasure at the quality of work the employee has been producing. Management's game is to get as much work as possible for no additional pay. Watch the men; for every new responsibility they accept there's normally a salary increment — so keep track of new non-routine duties and bring them up at performance-appraisal time.

If you work for several bosses and find you're getting bogged down by too many tasks, advise them that you can't do all the jobs today and ask which ones can be left until tomorrow. Know ahead of time what you *can* do within the usual business hours of your firm (don't add overtime as part of your regular day). Supervisors should be encouraged to place small coloured labels on the work they give out so their staff will immediately know what items are of first priority. Red is suggested for "urgent" (must be attended to immediately); yellow for "must be done today"; and green for "can wait until tomorrow." The supervisor should be sure to add a date and time to the tags, especially deadlines for red items.

When planning your day, don't plan every minute of it. There are bound to be interruptions and crises. You should plan approximately sixty to seventy-five percent of your day. It's a good idea to keep track of the interruptions and crises you normally handle in a week; that way you'll have a better idea of how much time you *really* do have for planned work.

If you don't practise time management and go on the way you are, you'll probably keep going faster and faster, but what will you end up doing? Making mistake after mistake after mistake. If you try to cram in all your duties, something's bound to happen to your accuracy rate. You'll hate your job more as time goes on. And it isn't just your present job it affects. Your manager's comment might be, "She can't even handle the position she's in, and she expects me to promote her?"

Women who allow people to dump on them are their own worst enemies. Learning how to say no, how to negotiate, and how to eliminate overtime is essential to your survival in business.

RULE 6: UNDERSTAND THE COMPANY HIERARCHY.

The office hierarchy (that is, the various ranks of employees) is usually defined on organizational charts. Have you seen the organizational charts for your company, or at least your branch or department? If you haven't, I urge you to try to do this, so you can see how your position fits in. The charts can also show you how to get where you want to go within the company. You'll be able to see who reports to whom and the status of each position. These lines to the top are important for your future. Although most lines appear to look progressive, if you check them carefully, only certain ones are part of the ladder to the top. You will also see that nowhere on that chart are clerical or secretarial positions shown, except as an adjunct to another position.

The title "assistant to" doesn't necessarily mean that you're in line for the position you're the assistant for. Nor does the title "office manager" always make you a real manager on your way up the ladder. This too is a dead-end position in many companies. Check it out before you choose a position with this title. See where the next step will lead you. These two positions could be compared to those of non-commissioned officers in the army. You'll seldom be given the chance to step on to the first rung, unless you obtain the same qualifications as the "commissioned officers." (This may require going out and getting additional training or education.)

Line Positions

There are certain types of jobs that lead to the very top of the ladder. Any operations job that involves the production of goods or services or the selling of these goods or services will get you there. These are in:

1. marketing (determining through surveys and research who and where the target markets should be);

2. sales (going to the target markets and selling the product or service to clients);
3. engineering and technology;
4. production (making the widget, or whatever the company sells);
5. contract administration (making a contract to sell or service a client and following the product or service right through credit checks, production, quality control, delivery, accounts receivable and accounts payable);
6. research and design (finding new products that the company can market. For instance, "We're making this kind of widget. How can we change it to hit another target market?").

These positions, all of which bring money *into* the company, are called "line positions."

Staff or Service Positions

Staff or service positions, on the other hand, *cost* the company money to maintain. They include positions in:
1. purchasing (buying goods from other companies)
2. data processing and computers
3. accounting
4. advertising
5. research (analysing why a product isn't working, rather than investigating new ones)
6. traffic
7. billing
8. industrial relations or human resources
9. medical services
10. legal services
11. public relations
12. credit services

You'll notice that women fill many of these positions, but few line positions. It's a sad fact that when a recession hits companies, staff positions will be eliminated before line positions are touched (as a human resources manager, I was one of the first to go). Also, managers in staff or service positions seldom make policy decisions.

If you're offered two positions at the same time, think carefully about which one is really the best for you. Let's say one is a promotion to a supervisory position (at a higher salary) with the staff department where you now work; the second is a lateral move (the job offers the same pay you are getting now), but to a line position. Which one should you take? After reading the preceding explanation, most people would say yes to the lateral line position. But, there's a further point to be made. On closer investigation, you discover the boss you would report to in the line position is one of the "incompetents" we discussed earlier. In that case, it would probably be better to get a promotion in your staff department and eventually try to land a position above the "incompetent." You might also have discovered that you will have less chance of obtaining a supervisory position in a line department, so you will be ahead obtaining the supervisory experience in a staff position.

Investigate all new positions thoroughly. You have to weigh all the facts. Keep up-to-date on what's happening in the line department of your choice and, when the timing's right, move in. Don't just jump at the first supervisory position open — weigh all the factors. It could be that you're in a position close to the top of your present department, so a move to the lateral line position might be the better move for you.

If you really want to forge ahead fast, work for a medium-sized company. There are fewer people to climb over, for one thing. Also, the smaller staff means you'll have to be more diversified. There's also more development of existing staff through necessity rather than choice.

On the other hand, if you want to know the most up-to-date way of doing something, work for a large progressive-thinking company. Their departments are normally broken down into more specific areas. To give you an example of this: in human resources I had to learn to classify jobs, so I worked full-time as a classification officer for a large company and stayed with it until I mastered it. Then I went on to learn about recruitment, performance appraisals, company benefits, exit interviews, training, etc., until I was truly a human-resources generalist. Then and only then did I have the diversified experience smaller companies required.

Have you determined where you would get the best training in your chosen field?

RULE 7: DIVERSIFY YOUR EXPERIENCE.

It's very important in business to have experience in as many areas as you can, both line and staff. But remember, always guide yourself into positions that lead to where you want to go. Before accepting any new appointment, ask yourself whether it's going to help you get where you ultimately want to be, or whether you are just floating and accepting whatever comes along. Become a specialist in at least one area, and keep your eyes open for what is going on in your company so you can pounce on opportunities as they arise.

RULE 8: DON'T SLIP INTO CARELESS WORK HABITS.

If you're bored to tears with your job, you may find that you do sloppy, careless work and pay little attention to detail and deadlines. If this is so, you're sabotaging yourself. You can't possibly be considered for a promotion because you're showing your superiors that you aren't ready for one. You can't blame them for thinking this. They see that you aren't even capable of correctly performing the tasks of your present position. Don't let yourself fall into this "Catch-22" situation.

RULE 9: WATCH OUT FOR THE MANAGER WHO ALLOWS SUBORDINATES TO BY-PASS YOU.

Be alert for the male manager who appoints you as supervisor but, under the guise of "helping" you, allows subordinates to by-pass you to obtain help directly from him. Your boss knows he's breaking a rule of the game, and he wouldn't consider doing so with a male supervisor. You can't allow this to continue. Bring the matter to his attention and show him how he's undermining your control. Ask him to send the subordinates back to you to settle their problems.

RULE 10: LEARN MILITARY TACTICS.

In the military, there are commissioned officers, non-commissioned officers and privates. Privates are part of the rank and file, ordinary soldiers without rank. They are at the bottom, below non-commissioned officers, which include sergeants and warrant officers. Commissioned officers are those ranks above warrant officer.

In business there's a very similar structure. Privates are clerical, secretarial and support staff. Non-commissioned officers are foremen and supervisors. Commissioned officers are managers and executives.

All of these groups operate according to certain *traditions* — sets of rules, many of which may be unwritten. Traditions often don't make sense, but traditional ways of doing things can often be the hardest to change. ("It's always been done that way!") It's women's job to try to change these traditions; but it won't be easy.

Very few privates ever manage to rise even to non-commissioned-officer's level; and very few clerks and secretaries make it to supervisor level. It's time to leave this tradition behind. Following the unwritten rules is one way for women to do so.

RULE 11: UNDERSTAND THE RELEVANCE OF TEAM SPORTS TO THE WORKPLACE.

It's not enough to be aware of the military-type code that prevails in business. You must also understand how the code of competitive team sports shapes corporate activity. Men understand team sports and enjoy a competitive atmosphere. The woman who has grown up with competitive *team* sports is very lucky. Most women have spent their time competing against themselves. I spent five years of my life competing in competitive sports, but in swimming rather than a team sport such as hockey. I was competing against myself, rather than belonging to a team that competed against other teams. It took me many years to realize I lacked an understanding of the rules of teamwork.

In talking with managers about how effective women were as team members, most related that women performed better when working by themselves. They were not as productive as men when involved in team projects, and seemed to lack the "team spirit" necessary for success.

What would happen if Wayne Gretzky of the Edmonton Oilers didn't know how to function as a team player? He's so good he could probably score most of the goals for the Oilers. But how would his teammates feel when he got all the glory? However, Gretzky's skills as a team player are considerable. When the opposition is following him, thinking he's going to make a slapshot, he passes the puck to a teammate who's not as well covered, and that player scores the goal. Through this kind of teamwork, the whole team benefits. When one individual tries to outshine the others, nobody benefits and teamwork fails.

When women rise to the management level, they must have "team spirit" and learn to work well with their male peers. They need to keep in mind that the whole team depends on them to do their work as part of a co-ordinated effort. Some women find it hard to work as part of a project team. They may neglect to check with their co-workers to see if there have been any major changes, or if they can supply some essential information needed to complete the project.

RULE 12: REMEMBER THAT TEAM PLAYERS CONFORM TO THE RULES, NOT THE RULES TO THE PLAYERS.

The United States and Canada play football by slightly different rules. When U.S. players join a team in the Canadian league, they have to play by Canadian rules; otherwise they're thrown out of the game. Women still have to conform to the established rules of the game in business; they cannot expect the rules to be adjusted to suit them (at least not yet). Women are slowly but surely making a difference as more of them get into management, but it will be a while before the rules change significantly.

If a player breaks the rules, she or he is penalized or held back. What would likely happen if you were the only woman in a team of men, and you let them see you were a lot better than they were? You'd be booted out. You can be a bit better, but it had better not be by too much or the others will sabotage your efforts. Then your manager will notice that you're not "one of the team" and get rid of you no matter how good you are!

This was one of the major mistakes I made. At one point I was handling three people's jobs at one time. This became necessary when two men in my peer group (who did essentially the same work I did) were absent for three weeks. I was the only one left to handle the work. The job was there, it had to be done, I seemed to be the only one qualified to do it, so I simply did it. What a mistake! I should have thought of the repercussions for my co-workers and asked for help from people in another division. (In fact, I would have burned out in the fourth week if I'd had to keep going at that pace.)

It didn't help to have my boss mention my feat to my co-workers when they returned. I wasn't aware of how threatening this must have been to them. They were obviously anxious that their jobs might be eliminated if one person could handle the whole case load. They were rightly upset and eventually made things rather uncomfortable for me.

Ask yourself if you've done this in the past, or — heaven forbid — if you're still doing it right now. If so, stop trying to be so much better than your co-workers. Be a little bit better, so your boss notices; but for the most part try to blend in with the rest of the team. This rule applies to both men and women. If you're at this stage, it usually means you are ready for a promotion.

The phrase that tells you you're *not* blending in with the team is, "You're making waves." If you hear someone *in authority* use that expression, be careful. You're stepping on somebody's toes, and you'd better stand back and look at what you're doing and whom you're offending.

Military language is used in business. Terms such as boondocks, boonies, flak, formation, jock, rank and file, scuttle-butt (gossip), sick bay, and the old favourite T.G.I.F. (Thank God it's Friday) all came from the military.

Sports lingo is everywhere in the business world too: (touch base, tackle the job, batting average, out in left field, coach, disqualified player, jock, team player, rules of the game, front line, ball-park figure, college try, pinch hitter, end run, huddle, good sport and bench sitter).

Another of these terms is "play your position." If your boss ever suggests you "play your position," he's probably saying: "Do your own bloomin' job!" To expand the sports analogy, he sees that your job was to play centre for that game, but you played defence, and he wants to know why. Men seem to understand that they have to play their position and no one else's, and they wonder why women don't do this.

In competitive sports, losing the "game" (failure at something you attempt) is a sign that more "practice" is necessary. Men know this. However, women often feel they have "failed" at something and take this "failure" personally. You must never accept defeat. Come back fighting. To men, there's no disgrace in losing while you're trying, but there is if you "give up the game," which they think of as the "sissy or girl's way."

RULE 13: KNOW THE STRENGTHS OF WOMEN IN BUSINESS AND LEARN TO USE THEM EFFECTIVELY.

Do you know what advantages women in management have? It has been said that women are more flexible and can accept change more quickly and easily.

Another advantage women appear to have is the ability to handle several things at one time. Because they've practised organizational skills in a multi-facetted home setting, they are better able to juggle competing tasks (as long as they have an organized boss who's not dumping all his or her excess information on their desks). What other advantages do you think they have? Here are some that I believe women have, which you may never have thought of as advantages.

LANGUAGE SKILLS

Scientific studies have shown over and over that women have much better verbal skills (oral and written) than men.

Communication skills

I talked about these earlier. They involve women's superior ability to read body language and their capacity for empathy. Keep using these skills. Improve them every chance you can by reading up on these topics. The better you read body language, the better you're going to be able to understand others.

For example: Your boss walks in. You see by his body language that he's having a *bad day*. You'll be able to say to yourself, "It looks as though he's having a *bad day*; I'd better stay clear of him." This skill of reading non-verbal clues is invaluable when dealing with family, subordinates, clients and co-workers. Body language very seldom lies. The spoken words of others should be disregarded if their body language is telling you something else.

The ability to put yourself in someone else's shoes and understand what they're feeling (empathy) is also invaluable. But beware: this skill is only useful if you can avoid getting too soft. Don't take on others' sorrows and troubles as your own.

For example, you've noticed that one of your subordinates is irritable and not producing the way she should on the job. Your empathetic skills enable you to determine that Mary's just having a *bad day*. You still need top production from Mary, however. You show empathy by saying something like: "Mary, I'm sorry things are going wrong right now, but I still need this report by four o'clock." This shows both understanding (you know she's having *a difficult day*) and strength (you expect certain things from her, whether she's having a *bad day* or not). Just the fact that you've acknowledged that Mary is having a rough time is often enough to change her behaviour.

Intuition

Women call it intuition. Most men call it a "gut reaction" or a "hunch." All of a sudden you have the feeling that you really should — or should not — do something, although you can't put a finger on why you feel *that way*. You try to establish facts that explain your feeling, but they just don't seem to come easily. I had it explained to me this way: When you get a flash of intuition, every single scrap of information in your brain is used to come up with the feeling. If you listen to your second idea (which is usually based on your conscious brain), you'll be using only a portion of all the information you have available to you.

Now, which one should you listen to? Of course! Listen to your intuition. When it tells you something — listen to it. It's seldom wrong. The only time I haven't listened to my intuition was when I took an instant dislike to someone. After standing back, I realized that this person physically resembled another person whom I disliked and distrusted. By turning off my intuitive feelings, I was able to learn that the person was okay.

I like to compare the brain to a computer. You're crazy if you don't use the best software available to you (your subconscious brain), because it has a memory bank far superior to lower-grade software (your conscious brain). When you listen to your intuition, you're using a superior memory bank. If you listen to only your second idea, you're using a low-grade or inferior memory bank. Doesn't it make sense to listen to the better one?

I've learned to listen to my intuition, and I'd like to give you an example of one situation that I get goose bumps just thinking about.

Years ago, when I was driving down a quiet residential street on a warm summer day in Winnipeg, I thought I saw a slight blur under one of the parked cars ahead of me, so I slowed down in case it was someone's pet. I was just about to pass the spot when my intuition took over and made me stop the car (beside the parked car). I looked around and still couldn't see anything. The uneasy feeling persisted, so I got out of the car to see what I could see. The next thing I saw has haunted me many a night — it was the sight of a baby crawling on the road in front of my left wheel! It would have been directly in front of my right wheel if I hadn't stopped when I did.

I looked to see where the baby had come from and retraced its path up a sidewalk, then up four concrete steps to a front door that was ajar. The baby had pushed the door open and had somehow crawled down the stairs.

I believe that listening to my intuition saved that baby's life. Think back to times you've used your intuition — and when you didn't, but should have.

Creative Problem Solving

A number of years ago, companies started using creative-problem-solving techniques. To explain: A problem is defined to a group; it then brainstorms and comes up with as many workable solutions to the problem as possible. One of the rules of brainstorming is that you have to offer your ideas without censoring them. No matter how silly the idea appears, it should be offered, because it may in turn trigger a better suggestion from someone else. Everyone in the room takes part, and one person writes down the ideas as quickly as possible.

This technique proved moderately successful until one day a manager who couldn't make it to a meeting sent his secretary to take notes for him. Since everyone was expected to participate, she was asked to contribute as well. The managers couldn't believe the outcome — she came up with two of the four workable suggestions. They couldn't understand why her answers were better than those of professionals who understood all aspects of the problem.

At the next meeting, an experiment was tried. All the managers were encouraged to bring their secretaries. Most of the ideas again came from the women. It seems that the women didn't censor their own ideas as critically as the men. The men generally questioned their ideas to see if they were good enough before submitting them to the group. Some did this out of a fear of looking silly, some because they couldn't turn off the self-censoring mechanism that told them, "That won't work."

In this case, the women had been told to let ideas flow unrestricted — so they did. They suggested any idea they could think of. It didn't matter whether it was a good idea because they had been told to be very open. And they were not as worried about looking silly.

If the men had practised listening to their "gut reactions" the way the women listened to their "intuitions," they wouldn't have had this problem. Many businesses now make sure half the participants in creative-problem-solving sessions are women.

Drive to Succeed
This is especially true of women who are getting into management, particularly ones who are coming back into the work force for a second career. Many of them have a tremendous drive to succeed, perhaps because they feel their major role in life (as a homemaker and mother) is probably over. They don't want to feel they're "over the hill," and they hate the emptiness in their lives. All the energy they once gave to homemaking and raising children they now expend in getting where they want to be in business.

Because they are "fresh," many have more stamina and enthusiasm than men of the same age, most of whom have been in the work force for fifteen or twenty years and have lost some of their momentum and zeal. Women in many management positions are keeping up a tremendous pace, which can be rather threatening to others whose momentum has slowed down. The men had this identical drive when they were twenty and first starting out, but they've forgotten the feeling. Women who've been in business all their adult lives also go through a slowdown. To keep interested and motivated, they should set new goals for themselves that are more applicable to their current needs.

RULE 14: DON'T DATE CO-WORKERS OR CLIENTS.
Can you anticipate some of the problems you would have if you dated someone you worked with, or a regular client of your company?

Most women believe this kind of arrangement is all right, that it doesn't affect their chances of success, but believe me it does. To be safe, stay clear of dating anyone you work with or have as a client. This is especially deadly if you work in the middle- or upper-management levels. Occasionally it might work out, but the odds are that it won't.

What causes most office romances? Proximity and availability. How much time do you think most husbands spend (awake) with their spouses? Married female employees spend just about the same length of time (often more) with male co-workers as they spend with their spouses. Beware of letting your hormones take over; think of the consequences after the romance breaks up. Inevitably, it will be difficult for both of you, but if one of you has to go, it will probably be the woman. If neither of you goes, it will still cause a serious strain on your relationship in the office.

It's amazing how fast co-workers catch on to the "office romance." You may think you've pulled the wool over everyone's eyes, but your body language will probably give you away. This kind of romance can be even more tragic if the person is your mentor (we'll be covering mentors in Chapter 13).

RULE 15: YOUR BOSS HAS THE RIGHT TO TAKE CREDIT FOR YOUR IDEAS.

Both women and men have been heard to say (I'll pretend the boss is male), "I worked all week on that report, and my boss took the credit for it — that's the last time he's going to do that to me!" When your boss "steals" your idea and takes credit for it, you've made him look good. And he needs you to do this. If you don't let him take the credit, he'll hold you back. This may still bother you. If it does, you could send your new ideas and suggestions to your boss in the form of a memo, asking his or her opinion about the merit of your idea. Then it's in writing. Or offer suggestions at a meeting where others know it's your idea.

It's a fact that he has the *right* (according to the existing rules of the game) to steal your ideas and do it with a clear conscience. According to business rules, you (the subordinate) are there to make your supervisors and managers look good. Most men and women dislike this rule, but the men abide by it. Your ideas become your boss's ideas, and he or she is not breaking any rules by taking credit for them. The funny thing is that male supervisors don't feel they're doing anything wrong because everybody does it. For instance, if you write a new policy and procedures manual for your department, your boss can take full credit for its contents.

However, when you yourself are a manager you should try not to perpetrate this practice. As I explain more fully in the chapter on supervisory skills (Chapter 9), it's a good idea for a supervisor to give credit where credit is due. If the subordinate has come up with a new method of making a widget, that employee *should* get the praise and recognition, not the boss. If supervisors keep stealing their subordinates' ideas, they demotivate their staff and will get only bad suggestions or no suggestions in the future.

RULE 16: LEARN TO USE THE APPEAL TO LOGIC INSTEAD OF TO EMOTION.

Men believe that the feminine trait of using emotions when making decisions is far inferior to their method of using "logic." However, many companies are spending a fortune teaching their employees transactional analysis and role playing, and are giving sensitivity training and pushing for better interpersonal skills — which suggests that they realize these "female" traits have their uses. But while men are being encouraged to be less logical and more emotional, women are being encouraged to rely less on emotion and more on logic and facts when making decisions. Perhaps we're looking forward to a nice mixture of these qualities sometime in the future.

Although these sixteen rules cannot cover all of the games played in business, these are the ones I feel are most crucial for aspiring managers and executives.

CHAPTER FOUR

CAREER GOALS

What is a career?
Many people are intimidated by the word "career," which conjures up the image of someone totally dedicated to work, someone with her nose to the grindstone all the time. If this image has put you off the idea of a career and prevented you from setting career goals, consider the following definitions — and then think again. A *job* is a position with specific duties and responsibilities. For example, teaching Grade 3 at Hillsdale Elementary School is a job. An *occupation* is a group of similar jobs in society. It's a broad category that may or may not be specific to a particular company, government department, organization, industry or profession (teacher, engineer, etc.). A *career* is the sum total of your work-related experience, including both paid and unpaid labour. Work-related experience includes full and part-time work, parenting and homemaking, volunteer and community work, hobbies and other leisure activities that may influence a person's work now or in the future. People may change jobs or even occupations, but each person has only *one* career. A job is what you do with your days — *a career is what you do with your life!*

The average woman works outside her home either part- or full-time for all but ten years of her adult life until retirement. That means that the average woman will spend approximately thirty-five years of her life working outside the home. Shocking, isn't it! So if you're in a boring job now, ask yourself how many years you have left to spend in a job you hate. You have two distinct choices — stay and suffer, or find something you like better.

Working at a career you're suited for can be tremendously stimulating. The work generates its own momentum, and you genuinely feel you are realizing your dreams. Often, you can't wait to get up in the morning. Mondays are great, and you start the day running. With this attitude toward your work you've a much better chance of progressing within the career you've chosen. The big question, of course, is how to find the career that suits you.

Do you have concrete career goals? From the time they're about eleven years of age, boys know how to answer the question: "What are you going to be when you grow up?" Ask most girls that age and they'll likely give you a blank look. They somehow don't think that this is an important issue for them. Usually these girls grow up having their parents set goals for them; later their goals are set in relation to husbands and children, not to themselves and their own needs and abilities. For women with this kind of background, learning to set personal career goals is a big challenge. But the results can make it well worth the effort.

HOW I OBTAINED CAREER COUNSELLING
In March 1974, I was lucky to meet a woman highly skilled in career counselling. She became a friend and offered me her expertise. After I had completed all the necessary psychological, IQ and aptitude tests, she suggested five occupations I could possibly excel at, with proper training. None of the professions suggested appealed to me.

I had "fudged" the test by answering the questions the way I thought she wanted me to rather than analysing carefully what was the truth for me. For example, one question asked whether I would rather be sitting behind a typewriter typing or fixing it with a screwdriver. The first time round I said I would rather be typing (I typed about 85 w.p.m.) when in reality I would much rather have been fixing it. I did the tests again, *the right way,* and thank goodness I did. It saved me many years of heartache that could have been spent in the wrong occupation. The five occupations that were then suggested to me were:
1.   Selling goods or services. Apparently, my persuasive powers were off the scale. At that particular time in my life, however, I

didn't believe I could sell my way out of a paper bag, so I said no to the choice of sales.

2. Marketing. That sounded great to me. Career counsellors, however, advise clients to speak to more than one person in each occupation chosen, as a safeguard against getting negative information from people who may be in the wrong occupation themselves (more than eighty percent of all people working are in the wrong job for them). I talked to several people in marketing and found that although it was a very interesting profession, it appeared to involve too much detail work for my liking. I decided not to go that route either.

3. Public Relations. After a bit of investigation, it appeared that this might be a suitable career for me. Then I learned there simply weren't enough jobs in Alberta to warrant taking the chance of being unemployed.

4. Human Resources (formerly called Personnel). This involved a variety of tasks — recruitment of staff, employee relations, job descriptions, classification of jobs, wage and salary surveys, performance appraisals, exit interviews, training and development. I decided to investigate my fifth choice before making any firm decision.

5. Small appliance repair person (believe it or not)! I knew I had an aptitude for mechanical and electrical things — but I had never thought of it as a career for me. That was too far out for me to consider in 1974, as there were very few women in such "non-traditional" jobs at that time.

After interviewing others and investigating thoroughly, I decided to pursue a career in human resources. I liked the variety it offered, as well as the people contact.

My counsellor wouldn't let me stop there. She explained that when you decide on an occupation, you have to set goals for yourself to achieve it. She taught me how to set long- and short-term goals. As I had never written goals for myself before, I found this quite a chore. Then she asked me to identify my specific goal in personnel. Did I wish to be a recruiter, to work in classification — what? After much soul-searching, I decided to go for the brass ring and aim for a position as head of a human resources department. (In 1974, there were very few women heads of *any* departments.) She didn't laugh. Instead, she encouraged me to chart a path so I could reach this lofty objective. I was encouraged to learn what education I would require and how I would obtain it; then, what kind of training and experience I would need to run a human resources department. I was encouraged to give time frames to my long- and short-term goals.

My first sub-goal was to find out what education would be necessary to get me where I wanted to go. With only a high-school diploma, was it likely I could be a company's human resources manager? Hardly. I opted out of going to school full-time and decided instead to take evening certificate programs (which consisted of ten, thirty-nine-hour courses each program). My first certificate program (Business Administration) was taken at Southern Alberta Institute of Technology in Calgary, followed by their Marketing Certificate, and later a Personnel Certificate at the University of Alberta in Edmonton.

Then, I had to learn what kind of companies would provide the best environment for in-house training. A job with a small company probably wouldn't be very effective in meeting my experience needs because most wouldn't have very sophisticated personnel systems in place. I decided the best environment would be in a medium-to-large company, where I could learn the most up-to-date systems. I would accept a position at a junior level and learn everything they could teach me — then go to another company and learn how they did everything. I learned that, like "skinning a cat," there are many ways to conduct personnel services — such as the different methods of writing job descriptions, evaluating positions and setting salary ranges.

Again my career counsellor gave me invaluable advice and recommended I set a backup goal as well. As she explained it, "Let's say you've planned and planned for a trip to Hawaii; you took the trip, and wondered why you had such a downer when you got back. It's because you had no backup goal waiting on the back burner for you to start working on when you were close to achieving your first goal."

When asked what my backup goal would be, I decided it was to have my own company to offer personnel services to companies too small to have personnel departments of their own. As I came closer to achieving my first goal, I was encouraged to develop a specific plan for achieving the second one, and to make sure that, as I went along, everything I did in my private and business life was aimed at achieving both goals.

Then I was urged to set time frames to these goals. I decided it would take fifteen years (until 1989) to reach my first goal of becoming human resources manager. My second goal — having my own company — I estimated would take twenty years (until 1994) to reach.

A strange thing happened to these goals. Because I knew exactly where I wanted to go, and how I intended to get there, I reached these goals long before I expected to! I had underestimated my abilities (as most women do). By 1980 (within six years of setting my goal — nine years ahead of schedule), I was appointed human resources manager of not one but a group of twelve companies. In 1982 (eight years after setting my goal — twelve years ahead of schedule), I opened my management consulting firm, Cava Management Consulting Services.

THE IMPORTANCE OF CAREER GOALS

When I was working as a human resources manager, a young woman came to me and explained that she was at the top of her clerical level and wanted to know what kinds of promotional opportunities there were for her with the company. I asked her where *she* wanted to go, what occupation she had chosen. She replied, "I don't really care what I get into, as long as it's a promotion and more money." I explained to her that she had gone as far as she could go as a generalist, that now she would have to specialize. She still didn't appear to understand what I meant, so I suggested careers in marketing, computers, personnel, accounting, sales, operations or production. She just shrugged her shoulders and repeated her original statement.

She failed to understand that companies don't just offer jobs to people; they have to have done something to earn them. She should have prepared herself for promotional opportunities, not expected her company to "find" the opportunities for her. For instance, if she wanted ultimately to be the purchasing manager of her company, she should have taken related courses in the evening so she would be ready for the next junior buyer's position that came up.

Goal-Setting Problems

Here are some goal-setting problems that have been related to me by participants of my Dynamic Goal Setting and Career Decisions seminars.

One woman had decided on an occupation but found that other occupations started looking good and overlapped with her original goals. Things were getting fuzzy. I explained that sometimes this happens. You might think, "Oh boy, would I ever like to be such and such." But until you really start investigating, you don't find out what the bad things are or what other opportunities are available in the area you've chosen. When I started the process of choosing a career, the best prospect seemed to be sales. Selling was what I ended up doing (conducting training seminars in which I'm selling ideas — one of the hardest things to sell). This is what counselling had pointed to all along. But I didn't start in sales; I wasn't ready for it right then. It was possible this woman, too, wasn't quite ready for the occupation she was best suited for. She might have to go around the periphery for a while until she gained confidence in her prime area of interest.

I suggested she make sure her supervisor knew where she wanted to go and ask for his or her help in getting there. If she didn't, her boss might assume that she didn't have career aspirations at all. I advised her to say: "I'm really interested in a career in this department. Can you give me some idea of my chances for getting promoted? Could you possibly help me learn the things I need to get ready for that next step up?" An empathetic boss would enable her to get the help she needed.

Here's a case in point. Andrea had worked for fourteen years with a company and had an outstanding reputation, but she was becoming bored and frustrated. She decided she had waited long enough. She approached one of the vice-presidents and asked where the company was going in the next five years and how she could help it get there. She told him of her accomplishments and employment record. Her timing couldn't have been better. He had been going over personnel files without much luck, and she turned out to be just the person he was looking for. He had never contemplated her for a promotion before (like most bosses he had just seen her as a woman, not as a potential executive). She was asked to open a new branch office for the company. This would not have happened if she hadn't spoken to a person in authority.

A part-time employee wanted to know if she could talk to her employer the same way. Certainly she could. For example, she could say, "I'm really enjoying my work here. Do you think there's any opportunity for me to be taken on full-time? Here are the areas I am interested in, and my ultimate goal is . . ."

In short, ask for help, rather than simply announcing what you want. Your approach is as important as your request. If you're just saying, "Hey, I need a better job, can you give me one?" you're unlikely to generate much interest. But if you explain what *you* have to offer, you'll most likely get a hearing.

Another woman set a goal — to get an accounting degree — came close to achieving it, and then found she was unhappy with her choice: "I'm finding that accountants are kind of boring," she reported. "I find I'm much more interested in management. Now I'm confused, because I've spent all those years toward something I don't want any more!"

I urged her to get career counselling to help her identify her transferable skills. Transferable skills (supervisory skills, interpersonal skills, accounting knowledge, aptitude with figures, scheduling skills, etc.) are those skills that can be taken from one occupational field to another. Her years of training could be of use elsewhere in many areas.

One client, who was working as a nursing supervisor, found she couldn't adapt to shift work and was worried she wouldn't be able to find work in any other occupation. I helped her determine what her "transferable skills" were. These consisted of such things as: an ability to supervise others; a knowledge of scheduling; highly honed interpersonal skills in dealing with all kinds of people from uppity doctors to querulous patients; an ability to keep meticulously detailed reports; an ability to remain calm in an emergency; physical fitness; an ability to make decisions quickly, etc. These were talents that could be useful in many, many occupations. She just had to find out which one she wanted to try.

Goal setting — intensive goal setting — is hard work. It takes a lot of effort and time. But *it's worth it*. If it takes you two years to decide where you want to go, that's okay, as long as you're steadily working toward finding the right occupation for you.

In the past, I've had the opportunity of helping many men and women with career counselling. One fellow, a mechanical engineer, had really made it in his field. But he almost had a nervous breakdown at the age of forty. He had met his goals, but had suddenly realized he didn't like what he had become or what he was doing! After counselling, he decided that selling would be ideal for him, but he was worried he would have to take a drastic cut in salary and that this would seriously affect the standard of living he and his family were accustomed to.

He was so close to his problem he couldn't see he would be literally a gold mine to some companies. I had interviewed hundreds of engineers and knew he had a unique talent. Many engineers admit they have trouble communicating their ideas either orally or in writing, but this man's communication skills were strong. I suggested he contact several firms that produce and sell technically difficult mechanical products to ask them if they required a salesperson with his background. He did so and, within a week, had five job offers.

Like many people who come for career counselling, he had no perspective on his problem and so couldn't see his own talents. (Try holding your hand an inch or two in front of your face. You can't see it clearly, can you? It's too close.) In career counselling, the counsellor stands back far enough to see things that individuals can't see for themselves.

Another client, a forty-year-old woman, consulted me when she was thinking about starting a "second career." She wanted to be an accountant, but she thought she was "over the hill and too old to learn." I asked her how many years she had to work until retirement. Twenty-five years, she said. Then I asked her my standard question: "Do you want to stay in a low-level, boring job until then, or would you rather do what *you* want to do?" She replied that she wanted to change but had reservations. "It'll take me four years of university to get the degree I need!" I asked her to consider how many years she would still be working after obtaining her degree. "Twenty-one years," was her reply. I asked her if the opportunity to spend twenty-one years of her life doing what she wanted to do would make the sacrifice of four years worthwhile. Her affirmative answer started her on the road to serious career planning.

At any age, you should be thinking about this, especially if you have been marking time in a job you dislike.

Being successful in your chosen career does take time, energy, dedication and effort. Don't go into something unless you really want to make a go of it, because you won't make it. There's too much competition out there — people who know where they want to go and how they're going to get there.

Think about the successful people you know. Did they put a lot of time, energy, effort and dedication into getting where they wanted to go? You'll probably find they did, because success doesn't come without all of those things. You have to be willing to put out that energy.

CAREER-PLANNING INFORMATION

There are four major steps in planning a career:

1. *Analyse what you like to do.*

You know what you like to do. Your career should allow you to do as many of those things as possible. You should feel as if you're "cheating" when you put your hand out for your paycheque because you're enjoying yourself so much.

2. *Analyse what you do well.*

Most people have difficulty identifying what they do well. If you have trouble with this, you might ask a friend to help you identify these areas.

3. *Match your interests and abilities to a job.*

The things you *like to do* are your interests. The things you *can do well* are your abilities. Write down these interests and abilities. You are now in a position to start your research.

Try to see your interests in terms of the work world. What work do you see others doing that really interests you? The best source of information about any career is the person working in the job. Ask if he or she will answer some questions relating to their position. You'll find most people love talking about their jobs and will be honest about things they like and dislike about their positions. If you don't know someone in the occupation, contact the heads of the human resources departments of companies that employ people in the kinds of occupations you're interested in. See if they can arrange for you to talk to some of their employees. Or you might work part-time in a position in your area of interest to learn about it first-hand.

Explore many occupations to determine what *you* like or dislike about them. Make notes of your observations for future reference. Read about what other people are doing. Would you like to do similar kinds of work? Even the want ads in the newspapers can give you ideas about the kinds of jobs available in fields that appeal to you.

In assessing any of these occupations there are two key questions you should try to answer: (a) What qualifications are required for this job? and (b) What promotional opportunities does the job offer?

4. *Decide what you want from work.*

Once you understand what you like to do, what you do well, and what types of occupations are suited to both your interests and abilities, consider the following questions, to help you determine what you want from your work:

- What working conditions am I looking for?
- Would I like the work itself?
- Will I earn enough money?
- Are the hours of work satisfactory?
- Do I have any physical problem I have to consider?
- Am I willing to travel on my job and/or work overtime?
- Am I willing to relocate?
- Am I willing to obtain further education and/or training?
- Will this job cause family problems?

As you look at different occupations, think about what each one involves (duties, responsiblities, working conditions, activities, etc.); what it requires from you (education, training, experience, personal qualifications); and what it has to offer you (opportunities for advancement, salary, benefits, skills). Then relate this information to your list of what you want in an occupation.

Keep narrowing your list down until you're ready to make a decision. This is a lifelong process. You could change jobs twenty times and work in five different occupations during your lifetime. Each decision you make will ultimately influence your career direction, but *you're the one who chooses the path.*

5. *Start the decision-making process.*

Next comes the goal-setting stage in which you set concrete short-term and long-term goals to help you obtain your "dream job."

Sample short-term goal: to complete one course (name of course) toward obtaining a Business Administration Certificate, with a mark of over seventy percent before December 4, 19__.

Sample long-term goal: to complete all ten courses of a Business Administration Certificate with an average mark of over seventy percent before June 19__.

All goals must specify requirements for quality, quantity and time (deadlines). You will want to plan where and when you will obtain the necessary training and/or education, what kind of company will provide the proper on-the-job training (if applicable), what knowledge you have to glean before being ready for the next step up, and so on.

GOAL-SETTING PLAN
When setting any goals for myself, be they life or career goals, I use the following plan to keep myself on track and make my goals far more concrete.

Step 1: Describe the situation as it is now.

Step 2: Describe the ideal situation.

Step 3: Identify the gap between 1 and 2 (the goal is to close the gap).

Step 4: List the driving and restraining forces.

Step 5: List ways you will overcome the restraining forces (brainstorm).

Step 6: Formulate plan of action.

Steps or actions	Date or time limit	People to involve	Resources required

Step 7: Implement your plan of action.

Step 8: Evaluate the success of implementing your plan.

NOTE: *Driving forces* describe the benefits you'll derive when you reach your goal.

Restraining forces are the things that may be in your way and may keep you from reaching your goal.

Goal setting will not get you that job. Putting your plan into action will. Don't allow yourself to get lazy; keep your momentum going by realizing that you're constantly moving closer and closer to your "dream job." Learn to be flexible, bounce with the punches, and keep your eyes open for unexpected opportunities to advance in your career.

CHOOSING A PROFESSIONAL CAREER COUNSELLOR
Should you wish help in career counselling, how do you select good professional help? This is a very difficult question to answer

because there are no officially accepted professional standards for most career counsellors. Unfortunately, not all career counsellors are equipped to help you, nor do many of them have the background to advise you fully. To choose a good counsellor, I suggest you spend time doing research to answer these questions:

– What background and professional training does this person have?

Post-secondary training in vocational guidance (not just personal counselling) is a good starting point. In addition, at least a year of work experience in an appropriate setting (e.g., educational institution, government agency) would teach this person to apply his or her learning to real-life situations.

– What do this person's past clients have to say about his or her career-counselling experience?

Legitimate agencies and/or private career counsellors will supply a list of past clients (with their permission) for references.

– How flexible is this person's approach to career planning?

Promoting only one route to career satisfaction or a very narrow selection of tests/tools could be a sign of professional rigidity or incompetence.

– Does this person appear knowledgeable and current about today's labour market?

The only way a prospective career planner can be assured of finding a *good* career counsellor is to learn the basics of career planning (by reading any of a number of excellent career-planning books available from colleges, universities and government agencies) and to be willing to ask why the counsellor is suggesting certain activities or exercises. Shopping around until you feel right about the counsellor's personal style and attitude is also perfectly acceptable.

Knowledgeable career counsellors will know what qualifications are required for different positions, and where this training can be obtained, be it through full-time study at a college or university, evening courses, or correspondence courses. Often companies provide on-the-job training; counsellors should know which companies do so.

There are many tools or tests that can be used in the first phase of the career-counselling process to gather information about your aptitudes, abilities and preferences. These include such things as:

Aptitude tests, which try to predict how you would do in certain ability areas (e.g., reasoning, verbal, formal, perceptual).

Interest tests, which try to measure what you like to do based on your past experiences and your personality (e.g., working with tools versus working with people).

Values inventories, which try to assist you to clarify and then rank your life-career values (e.g., the kind of work setting you want, the amount of energy you want to put into your work).

Skills inventories, which try to assist you to clarify and rank the work-related skills you already have. The focus is usually on transferable skills that are useful in more than one occupational setting (e.g., communication skills, budgeting skills).

Personality tests, which try to assess and categorize your overall personal characteristics. This is the most nebulous kind of test and most open to bias on the part of the counsellor.

These tests usually must be administered, scored and interpreted by a testing specialist or trained psychologist. These trained professionals will be able to determine which tests show sex biases in their questions. Sex bias is defined as any factor that might influence a person to limit — or might cause others to limit — his or her considerations of a career solely on the basis of gender. The perceptions of both client and counsellor have to be unbiased. If used carefully, standardized vocational tests can expand the choices, even if the tests contain some degree of sex bias, provided the counsellor is aware of the problems in the test. For example, if the pronoun "he" is used, or if such terms as "salesman," "policeman," etc., consistently appear, the test is probably biased and will not give a correct reading unless the counsellor is aware of the implications of the testing device. (The use of "she" when referring to such traditionally "female" occupations as secretary or nurse is another such indication.) The counsellor's own personal beliefs also influence the testing process and must be taken into account. If the counsellor appears to show bias against women, I suggest you find another counsellor.

For those contemplating a change in occupation, I recommend you also obtain help in preparing your résumé. Unless you really know how to put a résumé together, your qualifications may not appear to their best advantage. On average, more than 100 people apply for every advertised position — sometimes more. The only thing that sells your unique talents and gets you in the door for an interview is your résumé, so it's *got* to be good. I'm an advocate of the "custom-made" résumé — I recommend writing a separate résumé for every job you apply for. Read the advertisement carefully to determine what the company is looking for. If the ad asks for a self-starter, you'd better give reasons why you *are* a self-starter. Do the same for every request or qualification asked for. Give the employer exactly what he or she wants (but don't lie).

GOVERNMENT-SPONSORED CAREER CENTRES

In Canada, the following government agencies assist clients with career counselling. Normally these services are free. Contact these head offices to find the office nearest your town or city:

Yukon
Advanced Education and
Manpower
Department of Education
P.O. Box 2703
Whitehorse, Y.T.
Y1A 2C6
(403) 667-5131

Northwest Territories
Department of Education,
Advanced Education
3rd floor
50 Ave. and 49 St.
Yellowknife, N.W.T.
X1A 2L9
(403) 873-7553

British Columbia
Department of Labour
880 Douglas St.
Victoria, B.C.
(604) 387-3758

Alberta
Alberta Career Development
and Employment
10924 119 St.
Edmonton, Alta.
T5H 3P5
(403) 427-5659

Saskatchewan
Employment Development
Agency
Room 345
Legislative Building
Regina, Sask.
S4P 3B0
(306) 787-5353

Manitoba
Department of Employment
Services and Economic
Security
357 Legislative Building
Winnipeg, Man.
R3C 0V8
(204) 945-4285 or 945-4173

Ontario
Ministry of Skills Development
13th floor
101 Bloor St. W.
Toronto, Ont.
M5G 1V7
(416) 965-8634

Quebec
Vocational Training
Department of Manpower
and Income Security
3rd floor
255 E. Cremazie Blvd.
Montreal, Que.
H2M 1L5
(514) 873-5776

Prince Edward Island
Human Resource Development
Department of Industry
Shaw Building
P.O. Box 2000
4th floor
Rochford St.
Charlottetown, P.E.I.
C1A 7N8
(902) 892-5495 — ext. 64

New Brunswick
Department of Advanced
Education and Training
416 York St.
Fredericton, N.B.
E3B 5H1
(506) 453-8264

Newfoundland
Department of Career Develop-
ment and Advanced Studies
Confederation Building
St. John's, Nfld.
A1C 5T7
(709) 576-2722

Nova Scotia
Department of Human
Resources Development
and Training
5151 Terminal Rd.
P.O. Box 697
Halifax, N.S.
B3J 2T8
(902) 424-5632

GUIDELINES FOR SETTING CAREER GOALS

1. Choose Your Career

The most important thing to remember when filling out tests and forms is that you can't "fudge" the answers — they all have to be answered *as things are, not as you would like to pretend they are.* If you distort the truth of your situation, you won't come up with careers that suit your unique talents and abilities. You have to evaluate your strengths, your weaknesses, and your likes and dislikes and to make many choices. After deciding on two or three choices — determine if there is a market for that career. Determine

your top career choice and talk to at least two people in that profession. Ask them:
– what they like about their job;
– what they dislike about their job;
– what an average day entails;
– how they got to the position they're in (what education and experience is necessary);
– if they had to do it all over again, would they still choose that profession?

2. Decide How You Will Get Into Your Chosen Field

When you've made a choice of career, use the GOAL SETTING PLAN on page 57 to decide how to get into the area you've chosen. This is where planning comes in. Don't procrastinate — do it now!

3. Find a Position

This can be through word of mouth or through answering an advertisement in the newspaper. Some find a position through employment agencies. (Employment agencies *don't* charge the applicant — they charge the employer — so apply at several, it won't cost you anything for their help.)

If you're answering an advertisement, circle the verbs or action words used, then use these action words in your résumé and covering letter — it will give you an edge over other candidates. Answer all questions asked in the advertisement. Recruiters look for similarities between your qualifications and the job requirements.

4. Apply for the Job

Many people don't like using résumés. Instead they rely on application forms and hope these will get them in the door for an interview. Unfortunately, this seldom works — so use a résumé that "sells" your unique talents and abilities.

5. Attend an Interview

Usually, the only thing representing you prior to an interview is your résumé. If it isn't adequate, you simply won't be asked for an interview. If you're called in for an interview, remember that you are there to sell yourself — don't let shyness keep you from "tooting your own horn." Know your strengths and weaknesses and be ready to discuss them with the interviewer. Have your facts clear in your mind, anticipate the interviewers' questions, have information handy that they may need. Make sure your physical appearance is neat and clean and that your apparel suits the position you are applying for. Never, under any circumstances, wear jeans or corduroys to an interview. Office workers are encouraged to wear apparel one step up from the position they're applying for.

THE MID-LIFE CAREER CHANGE

More and more people seem to be making career changes in mid-life. A mid-life career change occurs when you switch from an occupation you've been established in for a considerable length of time to a different one. We *choose* some mid-life career changes — others are *forced* on us. Making this change often involves leaving an established position to go to a junior or entry-level position, which may involve a significant loss in income. The individual may need additional training before he or she can even make the switch.

Whenever possible, never leave one position without having another to go to.

More often than not, mid-life career changes affect others. We may be well established, with a network of relationships, commitments, responsibilities and obligations to family and work, so making a change of this kind is difficult and complicated. Our burning desire for change is mixed with guilt feelings that we are imposing our needs on our families, and this may hold us back from making the necessary move. But time is running out! It may be now or never, and every day we spend at our present job is one day less that we have for doing what we really want to do. So panic starts setting in.

Mixed in with the guilt are fears and doubts about making the change; feelings of frustration if we are *not* working toward the change; feelings of uncertainty about whether to stay where we are; hopes about the promise of better things if we go. Like all change, this type of move offers opportunities for self-fulfilment, challenge and personal satisfaction. But change of any kind also has a way of making us feel vulnerable and unsure of ourselves. Even the most self-assured people are shaken by change, so the support of family and friends becomes more and more important to us. I urge you to seek their support during your career changes.

If you feel your own self-esteem is the problem, Chapter 10 will help you feel good about yourself and improve your self-confidence.

CHAPTER FIVE

SUCCESS STORIES

Setting career goals goes hand in hand with thinking about a wide variety of possible occupations. The more widely you let your mind range over the resources and options available, the more chances you have of finding the career that suits your unique combination of interests and abilities. The examples in this chapter of women across Canada who have excelled in their own areas of expertise may be helpful. Many of the women don't have university or college degrees; many are married, with children. After reading each woman's story, ask yourself: Are they doing something that would be of interest to me? Can I learn anything from the problems they faced and the methods they used to get where they are? This will help you find out if you could do the same.

WOMEN IN TRADITIONAL OCCUPATIONS
Many of these women came up through the ranks, left their clerical positions and ended up in managerial or executive positions, or started their own businesses. Several stayed with the original companies they started with.

Gwyn Gill is 49, a high-school graduate who joined the Royal Bank as a teller in 1964 at the age of 26. She worked her way up through the ranks until, in 1974, she was the first woman with the Royal Bank in Quebec to be appointed assistant manager of a busy downtown Montreal branch. In 1984, she pioneered an innovative car loan that is very attractive to the new car buyer because it reduces monthly payments and guarantees that the client can sell the car back to the bank for a fixed sum at the end of the term. The bank made her their second female vice-president that year (vice-president of organization, planning and development and corporate planning and productivity). In September 1987, another promotion followed, to vice-president of retail banking for Metro Toronto headquarters. Gwyn is now helping her daughter, Diana, plan her career at the Bank of Montreal.

Problems she faced: She had trouble obtaining after-school care for her daughter.

Sylvia Rempel, now 50, emigrated at age fourteen from Germany. She's now the owner of Sun Ice Ltd., a Calgary sportswear manufacturer that opened its doors in 1978. Her company designs winter wear that is sold worldwide. Her trademark is her V-striped collar. Sylvia started with seven used sewing machines and a dozen seamstresses. First year sales were $50,000; second year sales, $325,000! She moved her shop to larger quarters and began distributing coast-to-coast in Canada, then tackled the U.S. market. By 1986, she had 165 employees and was turning out six lines of outerwear. That year she also went public with her company but maintained two-thirds control. Her husband, Vic, has joined the company on the sales side. Sun Ice was a finalist among those nominated for marketing awards in the Canada Awards for Business Excellence in 1987. Her company also won the right to be official supplier of ski wear for the 1988 Winter Olympics in Calgary.

Problems she faced: Although her designs are copyrighted, Taiwan, Korea and Hong Kong have been flooding the market with look-alikes. Her company is suing.

Secrets of her success? Hard work — putting in sixteen-hour days, seven days a week.

Edith Leppard of Lethbridge, Alberta, is 63 and has a Grade 11 education. She considers herself a self-taught businesswoman. Her knitting hobby became a career when her favourite knitting shop in Lethbridge came up for sale in 1970. (At that time she was also contemplating whether she should accept a personnel-manager's position.) Edith decided to buy the store, which she called the Carousel Knitting Shop. Her husband helped with the financing. She opened her second shop in 1984; again financing was no problem, because her first shop was thriving. In 1986, Edith sold her larger store so she could have more time for herself and for travelling and visiting her family.

Problems she faced: "People seem to think if you own a business you can take time off whenever you want, but just the opposite is true. It seems like I always have something to do. There will always be sacrifices, demands and pitfalls in owning a business. Hours are long, vacations are short; there are staff conflicts, shoplifters, burglaries, even cantankerous customers; but being my own boss has far outweighed any of these hardships."

Secrets of her success? After seventeen years in the business, she has learned to provide good service (often clients become her friends), hire knowledgeable staff, and replace every piece of stock sold either singly or doubly as quickly as possible. She also had good child care — her mother-in-law was willing and able to baby-sit the children whenever Edith had to work.

Nancy Theimer, 54, a Montreal-born Toronto resident, stopped work in 1957 when the first of her four children was born. In 1974, when her youngest child was six, she began to work full-time in the social-work field and to take courses to improve her qualifications. She had to drop the course work temporarily because of job and family pressures, but picked it up again, and in 1982 obtained her Bachelor of Social Work degree from Atkinson College, York University.

In the meantime she had worked for the Ministry of Community and Social Services, where she was employed as a social worker at a mental retardation centre from 1974 until 1978. From then until 1987 she held the position of case co-ordinator, and in October 1987 became a counsellor with Vocational Rehabilitation Services within the Ministry of Community and Social Services.

Problems she faced: Nancy learned that she couldn't be "super-woman" and work full-time, take courses, care for her four children, and enjoy a family and social life as well — hence her decision to defer her course work at the college.

Secrets of her success? Perseverance (she returned to college to complete her studies), single-mindedness, and the ability to establish priorities. It also helps that she loves what she's doing. She describes her work as stimulating, challenging and personally rewarding.

Shirley Deneault started as a clerk in 1965 for the Credit Bureau of Montreal; between 1965 and 1976 she held several positions, including one in which she supervised approximately sixty employees. When the Credit Bureau became automated, she worked as supervisor of the evening conversion unit. Later she became manager and spent the next three years automating bureaus throughout Canada. In 1979, Shirley was promoted to director of her division. In 1985, the company's head office (in Atlanta, Georgia) transferred the Canadian administrative functions to Canada, and Shirley was promoted to her present position as vice-president of administration for Equifax Canada. Her goal is to attain the highest position available in the corporation. The only condition she imposes on herself is that she must continue to feel the work is fun.

Problems she faced: She looked younger than she was (still does) partly because of her tiny frame. Shirley overcame this drawback by proving she deserved respect.

Secrets of her success? Self-motivation is the key — setting goals and "going for it." She learned always to look at the positive side, at what she had accomplished, and to move on to other things rather than dwell on failures.

Lynda M. Austfjord, 37, started as a junior clerk typist with the Credit Bureau of Winnipeg. Later, she worked in secretarial, accounting, supervisory and eventually management positions. In January 1984, she was promoted to vice-president of marketing for the parent company, Acrofax Inc.

Secrets of her success? Lynda worked hard, tried to anticipate and respond to the needs of both her division and her company. Most important, however, she learned to trust herself and have confidence that she was making a valuable contribution to the company. Her bosses provided opportunities for her to grow and cared about her development. The people who worked for her were dedicated, loyal people who were not afraid to work hard. As a team they motivated one another to higher levels of learning and achievement.

Cathie Irwin, 44, joined the Bank of Montreal's corporate office as a computer programmer in 1966 at age 22, but by 1968 she was so bored that she quit and taught skiing in Switzerland. She returned to the Bank of Montreal as a computer programmer in 1970. By 1980 she headed a department in Toronto, where she taught personnel how to analyse information on its customers. In 1982, she was made vice-president of distribution and payments-system planning; in 1986, she was promoted to vice-president of electronic-funds transfer at the point of sale.

Problems she faced: She was frustrated when her mathematics and economics degree was ignored. As well, her first position (as computer programmer) paid her only $3,000 (a teller's salary), while males doing the same work made $5,500.

Secrets of her success? Cathie was the first woman and the first person with a degree in the department. She was in the right place at the right time and had the necessary knowledge when her bank became automated and a senior position became available.

Jane Pepino, 40, was raised in London, Ontario. She has a master's degree in law and is a partner in the legal firm of Aird and Berlis. She is a founding member of the Metro Toronto Action Committee on Violence against Women and Children. Jane is also Metro Toronto's first female police commissioner and was one of a group of advisors on women's issues to Prime Minister Brian Mulroney. In the spring of 1987, she was appointed one of the first two women directors of the National Life Association Co. of Canada.

Problems she faced: In the late sixties and early seventies, law was still seen as a very non-traditional job for a woman. Jane's biggest problem was a combination of gender; age (youthful appearance); juggling the demands of marriage, motherhood and her law practice; and coping with the "working mother guilts."

Secrets of her success? She worked hard, took advantage of the breaks, and had a mentor who assisted her in overcoming the then widespread reluctance among law firms to hire women. (Within two years of commencing practice, the mentoring relationship simply dissolved, since it was no longer required.)

Jalynn H. Bennett had a B.A. in economics but couldn't type when she started her job in 1965 as clerical assistant to the assistant investment officer at Manufacturers Life Insurance Co. in Toronto. Her starting salary was $75 a week. Jalynn left work in 1970 when her first child was born, then returned to work part-time in investments. In 1972, she returned to work full-time at Manufacturers. By the mid-1970s she was herself assistant investment officer. In 1985, she moved into the company's corporate office as corporate development vice-president.

Secrets of her success? A good education, plus on-the-job training. Her involvement in outside community commitments also provided skills very useful in the workplace. Good timing, the ability to recognize new opportunities, and a well-developed sense of humour were also important.

WOMEN WHO CHANGED CAREERS

Elaine Andrew, 38, started out as a physical education graduate at the University of Manitoba. She then moved to Toronto and made a complete career change, joining the Toronto West-end office of Investors Syndicate. She started "at the bottom," but by the end of her third year had earned a Chartered Financial Planner designation. Elaine is an accomplished goal setter. At the beginning of 1986, she set three goals she wanted to achieve at Investors Syndicate:

1. Join their Executive and Corporate Division;
2. Attain diamond ring status ($8 million in sales);
3. Be a sales leader (top twenty-five in company — she was seventeenth).

By year end, she had met all three goals (her sales were $9.5 million). She has new goals now! One of those is to be working within ten years' time, only with clients, rather than doing marketing.

Problems she faced: Adjusting to living off a commission (she was accustomed to having a regular salary) and having a baby in her first year were the main difficulties she had to overcome. As well, the financial industry is still dominated by men, and she had to put in long and trying hours to prove she was capable.

Secrets of her success? A very supportive spouse (she says she couldn't have made it without him), effective time management, the ability to present information in a very professional manner, and excellent service to her clientele.

Sandy Lewis, 44, a resident of Edmonton, was born in England and emigrated with her husband and small son in 1965. She feels that her diversity of employment experience was an asset. She worked in a clerical capacity from 1960-64, then took time off for her family until 1968, when she joined the banking industry. From 1979-83 she ran not one but three businesses: her own bookkeeping business, Sandy's Bookkeeping Services, in Whitecourt, Alberta; Design 8 Ltd., in both Whitecourt and Edmonton; and the Duke of Westminster, a 150-seat pub-restaurant in Edmonton. Her most "out-on-a-limb" endeavour was the complete interior design of a $7.2-million hotel. Since 1983 she has been employed in Edmonton as the marketing manager for a national credit organization.

Problems she faced: At first she felt that a university degree was necessary to succeed in business. However, time and experience showed her this was not the case. She describes herself as a perfectionist. Difficulties in balancing a career with being a wife and mother made her by-pass promotions if they involved long hours or required travel away from home.

Secrets of her success? "A common-sense approach to any task, enjoyment of my work, a keen desire to be the best I can be, never being afraid to tackle anything, and willingness to work long, hard hours to accomplish my goals. If you earn the respect of your peers, keep out of office politics, and do your job, everything else falls into place."

Claudia Echart changed careers after twenty-six years in the banking industry. Her last position there was as a bank manager. Claudia now works for the Oakville, Ontario, branch of Investors Syndicate. In 1987, Claudia, like Elaine Andrew, received diamond ring status for sales of over $8 million.

Secrets of her success? Treating her clients well, using empathy, and being willing to put in long hours (ten to twelve hours a day).

Margaret Leahey, 32, was born in Halifax, Nova Scotia, one of a family of seven children. She began her journalism career with the Irving-owned newspaper in Moncton, New Brunswick, working as a reporter, columnist and entertainment editor. She was then sixteen and still a high-school student in an enriched program.

After graduation, her full-time employment at the newspaper and her high scholastic achievements enabled Margaret to launch her career in television. After a season as women's director of the Atlantic Television System (ATV Moncton), she was promoted to news bureau chief in Saint John and Fredericton, thereby becoming New Brunswick's first female television reporter.

Political reporting soon became a specialty for Margaret. In 1977, she uncovered a major scandal in the Hatfield government. Her skills as a political reporter then took her to Alberta as senior political affairs reporter for Dr. Charles Allard's CITV television station in Edmonton. In addition to nightly news reporting, she also produced and hosted her own federal-provincial current-affairs program.

Margaret has won two national awards for excellence in broadcasting and was elected president of the Economics Society of Northern Alberta.

She launched her latest career in April 1986, when she was appointed chairman of Alberta's Advisory Council on Women's Issues. This fifteen-member council reports to the government on women's needs and concerns.

Problems she faced: Loss of privacy due to her high public profile.

Secrets of her success? "My parents instilled in me at a very young age a belief in the importance of contributing to society. I'm results-oriented and have always been a firm believer in the work ethic — to always do my best at everything I attempt. My father taught me to believe in myself . . . for without personal confidence I don't think I could ever have taken on the successive challenges I've had in my life."

WOMEN IN UNUSUAL CAREERS

Kathy Mallett, 39, was born in Winnipeg of Native-Canadian parents. She completed high school, then took various clerical jobs. In 1978, at age 29, she enrolled as a mature student in political science at the University of Manitoba. There she became president of the Indian, Métis and Inuit Student Association. Later she co-founded the Native Women's Society of Winnipeg, and worked to establish a housing co-op for single mothers and their families. In 1985, she won the Winnipeg YWCA Woman of the Year award for community service. Kathy is the driving force behind the Winnipeg Coalition on Native Child Welfare, which lobbied the Manitoba government to allow the Native community to care for its own children from troubled homes. She works with young people and women in trouble with the law.

Deborah Mearns also wanted to help her own people — Native Canadians. She felt the best way to do this was to become a lawyer. She was president of the Vancouver Indian Centre for three years. As such, Deborah negotiated with the Ministry of Human Resources and with local banks to build the centre. She was also responsible for developing housing facilities, a task that included acquiring a hotel and other residential properties for Native people. She has established two Native group homes, a day-care centre, a restaurant and a construction company for Native people. Deborah is also a member of the Native Indian Child Welfare Advisory Committee and the Canadian Indian Lawyers Association. She's a director of the Native Court Workers Association, the Downtown Eastside Community Health Society, and the Grandview Woodlands Area Council. She was nominated for the Vancouver YWCA Women of Distinction awards in 1987.

Shirley Chan, 40, is executive assistant to the president of the British Columbia Institute of Technology, a director of Vancouver City Savings and Credit Union and English secretary to the Chinese Cultural Centre Board. From 1971 to 1981, she worked in various capacities for the federal public service. She also earned a Master of Environmental Studies degree from York University. Shirley became involved in community service when she helped stop the demolition of Gastown, Chinatown and Strathcona in Vancouver and started a movement across Canada for neighbourhood preservation. From 1981 to 1986 Shirley was executive assistant to the mayor of Vancouver, serving as policy advisor and chief of staff. She was also nominated for the Vancouver YWCA Women of Distinction awards in 1987.

Problems she faced: Always being mistaken for a secretary and the need to assert herself as a professional.

Secrets of her success? Her husband, Stephen, gave up his job to stay home and care for their two young children, which allowed Shirley to pursue her career.

Moyra Jones has been employed in the health-care industry for twenty-five years. She now works tirelessly and selflessly to increase public awareness about Alzheimer's disease, and to educate family and professional care-givers in creative-problem-solving techniques for persons with mental disorders. She was instrumental in arranging Vancouver's first conference on Alzheimer's and, as a board member of the Alzheimer's Society, helped establish Alzheimer's support groups throughout B.C. Moyra also produced the documentary *Unraveling,* a look at the disease from the perspective of victims and family members. She travels extensively, lecturing and developing programs for Alzheimer patients. She is currently working on a book on the subject. She was also nominated for the Vancouver YWCA Women of Distinction awards in 1987.

Secrets of her success? Supportive friends and colleagues, plus a husband and son who kept telling her: "You can do anything you want to do!" She had great mentors, but they were usually men who gave her a leg up (she often saw women being very cruel and uncaring to each other).

The next two women pooled their resources and now work together in Calgary.

Helen Vanderburg, 29, has a bachelor's degree in physical education from the University of Calgary. She earned gold medals for Canada in synchronized swimming at the Pan American, Pan Pacific and World Games of 1978-79. In 1979, she was selected as Canada's Female Athlete of the Year and also became a member of both the Canadian and the International Sports Hall of Fame. Helen then worked as a fitness trainer in Calgary and Vancouver, giving lectures and workshops for the public-school board and the University of Calgary.

Joan Santopinto, 34, also has a bachelor's degree in physical education from the University of Calgary, and has done graduate work in exercise physiology in the United States. She has developed fitness programs for private clubs in Calgary, and competed in marathons in Boston, Seattle and New York.

In 1982, with Helen Vanderburg, Joan opened Heavens Fitness Ltd., a health club in Calgary. Their aim was to increase the level of professionalism in the fitness industry and offer safe but motivating aerobic workouts to their members. They initiated low-bounce classes for people with knee or back problems. They also offer classes for two- to five-year-olds. They have been invited to Hong Kong to help increase public awareness of and participation in aerobics in that city.

Problems they have faced: Initially they had little knowledge of business or management and faced a very competitive market. They work long hours, seven days a week.

Secrets of their success? The ability to be constantly improving the quality of both their workouts and their staff. Sending questionnaires to their clients helps them keep up with clients' needs. To keep learning, they also attend major sports-medicine and aerobics conferences in the States.

Jacqie Shartier, 39, saw a market for a business in Canada that wasn't being tapped and opened a company in Edmonton called Balloon World. She was right, and her first year in business (1984) brought in sales of $84,000. In 1985 sales were $234,000, and in 1986, $500,000! Jacqie soon hopes to crack the Australian market.

Problems she faced: She had trouble obtaining financing when she needed to cover purchase orders of clients.

Secrets of her success? Good business ethics, which she learned from her mother, who stressed, "You can be what you want to be as long as you keep your name and service good — keep a good work ethic."

Viola Marie Robinson was orphaned at the age of thirteen, married young and left high school after Grade 11. In October 1974, Viola had a husband and six children, resided in a small home and was having a very difficult time financially. She realized that there was something very wrong with the system. She was a Native-Canadian but had no access to services provided by the Department of Indian and Northern Affairs until a friend mentioned the term "non-status Indian." After many telephone calls, she learned that there were many other off-reserve Native-Canadians in the same situation across Canada. She contacted the off-reserve population in her immediate area and received their endorsement to write a grievance letter to the Status Indian Association. When a general assembly meeting was set up in Yarmouth, Nova Scotia, she was selected to present their issues.

In June 1975, she was elected president of the Native Council of Nova Scotia, which represents the off-reserve aboriginal people of that province (Micmac) and those of aboriginal ancestry (Métis).

Since that time she has taught herself how to communicate and comprehend policies at all levels of government and now plays a leading role in educating the public on aboriginal issues.

Problems she faced: Making the transition from being a house-wife to handling a managerial position that required a lot of national and international travel was very difficult for her. The unpredictability of the demands on her time was also initially hard for her family to adjust to.

Secret of her success? The support of her family and friends.

WOMEN IN NON-TRADITIONAL OCCUPATIONS

Cathy Anderson was born in Winnipeg to Canadian Forces parents. At age 22 she obtained a nursing degree from Saskatoon's University of Saskatchewan, then earned a B.A. in sociology at 32, and is now completing her M.Sc. in social and preventive medicine. Cathy left the female bastion of nursing and is now responsible for the prevention and control of Saskatoon's infectious diseases, ranging from measles and flu to S.T.D.s (sexually transmitted diseases). She frequently lectures to medical students on the topic. She has spearheaded a unique data-entry system to track the incidence of S.T.D.s.

Problems she faced: Proving that as a nurse she was capable of handling the senior position of epidemiologist for the City of Saskatoon — a position traditionally filled by a male physician.

Secrets of her success? Having the foresight to recognize the need for a local expert on infectious diseases and persevering in attempts to prove she was the person to fill the vacancy.

Lucille Johnstone, 62, had to defy her parents and grandparents to complete high school. To pay for her books and clothes she held after-school jobs while earning her diploma. She earned an accounting degree at night school during the fifties. Lucille started work as a Girl Friday with RivTow Straits Ltd., a Vancouver-based marine-transportation, shipyards and heavy-equipment-distribution company. She worked her way up through the ranks to become, in 1970, vice-president of administration. She later was appointed senior vice-president of administration and company secretary. By 1985, this company had 1,500 employees and annual sales of over a quarter of a million dollars. Like many other successful women, she's very visible in the community. Lucille is a director of B.C. Place, the Northland Bank, B.C. Resources Investment Corp. and Hiram Walker Resources.

Secrets of her success? She learned how to research whatever she needed to know by asking questions and reading up on the subject.

Rosemarie Kuptana, 33, was born in an igloo to parents who were hunters and trappers. She quit high school in Grade 12 and worked both for Inuit political groups for the Sachs Harbour settlement council and as a CBC Radio announcer before joining IBC (Inuit Broadcasting Corp.) as a production co-ordinator. Since 1983, Rosemarie has been president of the IBC, which produces Inuktitut television programs that are distributed by satellite to Inuit communities. As president, she is responsible for a $2.2-million budget.

Stella Thompson obtained a master's degree in economics during the late sixties. She is married, with one son. Her husband is a professor at the University of Calgary medical school. Stella worked her way up through the ranks in the oil patch. Only two percent of Petro-Canada's upper-level managers are female, and Stella is one of them. She's presently general manager of product supply of Petro-Canada Products for the western region.

Secrets of her success? Twelve hour days, plus time on the weekends as well.

Brenda Malkinson, 35, a graduate of the Alberta College of Art in Calgary, now lives in Edmonton. She started a one-person stained-glass studio in 1975, which she incorporated in 1980 and called Lady of the Glass and Co. Ltd. She developed a gallery, sold retail and wholesale craft supplies, and offered glass-making classes. She does all the design work herself but hires occasional outside help for leading and assembly work. In 1982, she closed her storefront studio and worked out of her home, cutting her overhead by one-third. In 1985, she moved her studio to the Municipal

Airport, Hangar 3, and changed the name of her company to B.G. Malkinson Designs Inc. Her largest project so far has been a three-window commission for the Alberta Government's travel information centres in Lloydminster, Canmore and Walsh.

Problems she faced: Inexperience in running a business. She learned along the way.

Secrets of her success? Her positive attitude, stubborn optimism, loyal friends and supportive clients. With integrity as her watchword, she created the best designs possible, put in long hours to meet deadlines, and worked to maintain a businesslike attitude without sacrificing creativity. She borrowed as little as possible and had very accurate projections of where her business was going.

Dianne Mirosh graduated as an RN and worked as a nurse with Wescan Health Services, which provided insurance medicals. The job gave her the knowledge she needed to start her own business. She faced her biggest challenge as the first woman board member of the Hospital District No. 7 Auxiliary and Nursing Home Board. Until that time it had been an all-male board. Two years later, Dianne was appointed the board's vice-chairman.

In 1979, working with little more than a good idea, she opened her own mobile health service in Calgary called Access Paramedical Ltd. The company does audiometric- (hearing), visual- and pulmonary-function testing of employees at their work sites. This mobile health unit meets the demands of client companies who want to avoid the expense and lost hours of sending employees to medical-testing centres. At first, Dianne worked out of her home and a neighbour answered her phone while she was out on calls. Within three months, she had hired her first additional nurse, and by 1985 she had thirty employees. She now calls her company Access Occupational Health Services Ltd., has branch offices in Red Deer and Medicine Hat and a clientele of more than a hundred companies.

Dianne wasn't through with trying new things. In June 1986, she faced new challenges when she was sworn in as the MLA for Calgary-Glenmore!

Problems she faced: Her first loan needed to be co-signed by a man — her husband. (She got her second loan on her own through a federal government loan of $15,000 at one-half prime plus one percent interest for five years. She recommends that women enquire about and take advantage of government grants.)

Secrets of her success? She enjoys her work. Enthusiasm and the day-to-day gratification of her job keep her going. She's flexible, patient, and willing to listen to clients and staff; she's available for problem solving, and has kept up with new technology. She believes in full community involvement, which is valuable in her current position as MLA. "Successful entrepreneurs," she says, "must be willing to work hard, put in long hours and have constant people contact."

As these examples show, adopting an adventurous and optimistic attitude when setting your career goals can pay off.

CHAPTER SIX

HOW TO OBTAIN THE SALARY YOU'RE WORTH

EQUAL PAY FOR WORK OF EQUAL VALUE

"And the Lord spoke unto Moses, saying, 'Speak unto the children of Israel, and say unto them: . . . Thy valuation for the male from 20 years old even unto 60 years old, even thy valuation shall be 50 shekels of silver, after the shekel of the sanctuary. And if it be a female, then thy valuation shall be 30 shekels.' " (Leviticus, 27:1-4)

Equal pay for work of equal value was obviously not practised in Biblical times and has not been practised since. Changing this value system will be a slow and time-consuming process.

Women across North America have been fighting for wage parity for many, many years. Most people believe that the principle of equal pay for work of equal value means that a man and a woman doing essentially the same kind of work should receive equal pay. But there's considerably more to it than that. The laws of seven provinces already provide for equal pay for similar or substantially similar work. And this applies to both the private and public sectors. However, we still do not have pay equity. Why?

Many employers have highly developed job-evaluation schemes that they insist provide equality for all. When formal job-classification systems were established decades ago, it was assumed that all work done by employees would be evaluated fairly. Salary ranges were chosen that were said to be fair for the duties performed. This scheme involved assigning points for factors such as knowledge, skill, effort and working conditions. On the surface, this is what classification systems do. However, the criteria for assigning *merit* or importance to each kind of task is terribly out of whack. Lower salary ranges are usually assigned to traditionally female positions, and discrimination is the result.

In many companies you'll find that only a small segment of employees (the middle group) has been evaluated fairly by their company's evaluation system. If lower and upper level positions are examined, it's often found that incorrect salary ranges have been allotted. Lower people are underpaid and upper people are overpaid! No wonder there is such resistance to pay equity by upper level decision-makers in industry.

If these old job-classification systems had been implemented correctly, women working in secretarial positions would have been paid as much as technicians because of their specialized knowledge and skills. Many secretarial positions require the same length of training as technologists' jobs. However, this is not reflected in the salary structures for the two types of jobs.

Until recently, women accepted this type of inequity as their lot. But this is changing. It has to. As women understand business practices better, they learn that companies simply can't run without efficient support staff. However, many businesses believe that legislation to bring in equal pay for work of equal value — that is, to equalize the salary structures for *different* but equally important jobs — will cripple their companies. In a way, you can't blame companies for opposing such legislation. They believe they cannot afford to implement this policy in a tight economy.

IMPLEMENTING PAY EQUITY
The pay-equity laws differ in key categories among the Canadian jurisdictions that have them, or will have them.

Scope of Legislation
Some laws apply to all federal employees and to Crown corporations. In Quebec and Ontario, there are laws that apply (or will apply) to the public sector and the private sector (including companies regulated by legislation). In Manitoba, the public sector only is affected.

Model Used
The model is the underlying method by which the pay-equity law is to be applied. In federal government jobs and in Quebec, a complaint must be lodged by the employee. In Manitoba and Ontario, the employer must take action to comply with the law.

Definitions of "Value" (Criteria/factors)
To determine the value of a job, criteria for assessing value have to be defined.

In federal government jobs and in Manitoba and Ontario, a combination of skill, responsibility, effort and working conditions is examined to determine the value of a job.

In Quebec, the term "equivalent work" is used to refer to equal pay for equal work, for substantially similar work, and for work of equal value. "The jobs need not necessarily be identical, but a high degree of similarity must be demonstrated" in the skill and effort required, in responsibility and in working conditions. All four of these criteria need to be satisfied before two jobs can be deemed "similar."

Comparability
Federally, both female-to-male and male-to-female comparisons of employees and occupations may be made. In Manitoba and Ontario, comparisons may be made only between female dominated and male-dominated job classes. In Quebec, comparisons are not restricted by gender.

Definition of gender predominance
In the various laws, a position must first have a specified number of males or females predominating in the position before comparisons can be made. For federal employees, the occupation must be at least seventy percent male or female dominated in groups of up to 100; at least sixty percent in groups between 100 and 500; and at least fifty-five percent in groups of 500 (groups are occupational groupings). In Manitoba, a job class with ten or more incumbents must be seventy percent or more male or female dominated. (All other situations are as negotiated or to be defined in regulations.) In Quebec, the percentage is not specified in regulations or guidelines; and in Ontario a job class must be sixty percent female dominated or seventy percent male dominated to qualify for re-

evaluation. Employers must also consider historical incumbency and gender stereotyping.

Definition of establishment

All laws apply only to an "establishment," which is defined differently by each of the three jurisdictions in Canada. The pay equity plans of the federal government and Ontario are geographically defined (within certain geographic boundaries). In Manitoba, the process of implementing pay equity for civil-service employees must have commenced by October 1, 1985; for crown entities and external agencies (Manitoba's four universities, twenty-four of the largest health-care facilities and personal-care homes) by October 1, 1986. Employees who work for a company at more than one location within Quebec would be paid the same, providing it was established that they were in what is defined as "similar" positions.

Reasonable factors justifying pay differences

While pay-equity laws aim to eliminate glaring discrepancies in benefits and wages for undervalued workers, certain "reasonable" factors that justify differences may be taken into consideration.

Federally, these include different performance ratings, such as seniority, red circling, rehabilitation assignments, demotion-pay procedures, phased-in wage reductions, temporary training, labour shortages, and changes in the nature of the work performed. In Manitoba, individual factors justifying pay differences may be negotiated on a case-by-case basis.

In Quebec, such differences are not regarded as discriminatory if all personnel are judged on the following criteria: experience, seniority, years of service, merit, productivity and overtime. In Ontario, such factors as a formal seniority system, a temporary training assignment, a merit-compensation plan based on formal performance ratings, red circling, and skill shortages that cause temporary inflation in compensation are justifiable reasons for differences.

Phase in — Back Pay

The laws may indicate when employers must have in place their own equal-value policies, or how much back pay must be awarded to successful complainants.

Federally: law legislated in 1977, and section II came into force on March 1, 1978. There is a limitation period of one year prior to the complaint.

In Manitoba, two years are permitted for job evaluation and union negotiation and four years for implementation. Compliance in the public sector is required one year earlier than in the broader public sector.

In Quebec, compliance in the private and public sectors was required on proclamation of the legislation in June 1975.

In Ontario, timelines were set out as shown in Table 6:1:

Table 6:1

	Number of employees	Pay-equity plan and postings in workplace	Wage adjustments
Public sector		2 yrs.	2 yrs.
Private sector	500+	2 yrs.	3 yrs.
	100-499	3 yrs.	4 yrs.
	50-99	voluntary	5 yrs.
	10-49	voluntary	6 yrs.

Monetary limit

Federally and in Quebec, there is no ceiling on the amount of compensation that may be sought. In Manitoba, an award of up to one percent of the previous year's payroll per year over four years may be claimed. In Ontario, public-sector employees may claim up to one percent of the payroll per year over seven years; private sector employees may claim up to one percent per year until pay equity is achieved.

Not all provinces have yet taken steps to implement pay-equity laws. And of those that have, some limit actions under the legislation to cases of gender discrimination or female-dominated occupations.

Businesses should be encouraged to implement fair classification systems for *all* positions. The position, "not the person filling it," should be evaluated. Business owners contend that they can't afford to make these essential changes, but an imaginative approach to the problem would enable them to do so. Those who've been overpaid according to fair and realistic job-evaluation criteria could have their salaries frozen, and those whose positions have been undervalued could be paid a regular salary increase plus a portion of the increase that would normally go to the "frozen" employee until equity is achieved. Companies would not lose money under such a scheme.

One example of pay inequity came to my attention when I was employed with the Alberta attorney general's office in 1978-79. I conducted interviews to hire staff for its offices all over the province. At that time, there was a high turnover of judicial clerks. When I looked at their job descriptions, I realized why this was occurring. Although they had the title "clerk," many were performing the duties of an office manager or department head. The job description of a Judicial Clerk III read in part as follows: "May act as Deputy Clerk or Deputy Sheriff; supervise, co-ordinate activities, direct preparation and maintenance of police court records; direct all seizure proceedings; direct sheriff's sale proceedings; direct and approve searches made in the Sheriff's office; act as Vital Statistics Registrar. Supervision received is very general in nature." In many cases, these employees literally ran the court offices. Also, in many rural areas, when these clerks (mainly women) went on the circuit with the judges, they were required not only to collect fines (which could be for considerable amounts often in cash), but also to carry evidence for the trials. This evidence could include such things as illegal drugs or alcohol, or confiscated weapons. These clerks often travelled alone to the different judicial offices and had no weapons to protect themselves.

A judicial enquiry into this situation was begun in the early 1970s, and the necessary adjustments were (finally) implemented after completion of the Kirby Report in early 1982.

PART-TIME WORKERS
Part-time workers, almost three-quarters of whom are women, are also fighting for fair wages and benefits. In every occupational category, part-time workers receive lower pay than full-time workers. This is one of the main reasons why eighty percent of unemployed women want full-time, not part-time work. Full-time

employees' company benefits often add up to thirty percent of their salary (or more). Part-time workers believe that these benefits should be prorated, based on the number of hours worked. At present, part-time employees receive at best six percent vacation and statutory holiday pay. However, many of these "part-time" workers put in as much as forty hours a week, with no company benefits! Their employers are getting a free ride at their expense.

Discrimination in wages still persists, and women must fight if they wish to get out of the pink-collar ghetto. As it stands now, women are subsidizing businesses, and this has to change!

According to Jane Bryant Quinn (*Woman's Day*, March 4, 1986), "The average woman earns approximately $0.69 for every $1 earned by men." If a fairer job-evaluation system were used, this would be about $0.80 for every $1 earned by a man.

A variety of excuses is given for paying women less than men. It may be assumed that a married woman doesn't need a high salary, but that a man with "a family to support" should be paid more. The assumption is often made that a divorced woman is receiving huge alimony or child-support payments, or that a single woman's "dates" pay for all her entertainment. But whether or not a woman has a man to lean on financially — and many do *not* — is completely beside the point. The state of an employee's personal life has nothing to do with what he or she should be paid to do a specific job. If your employer throws these outdated excuses at you, defend yourself. Women pay rent, utilities, income tax and so on, just as men do, and they have a right to expect comparable salaries.

HOW TO GET THE SALARY YOU'RE WORTH

Women who want equal pay for work of equal value must learn to stand up for themselves and negotiate the salaries they're worth, just as successful men do. And they must look at the full package deal, not just the salary. This includes extended holidays, a larger office and support staff. They should make sure their company pension-plan benefits are the same for women as men.

Companies normally offer a woman a lower salary than a man, so before you go to an interview, do your homework; determine the salary range of the position you're applying for. Get this information by phone from the company representative who's responsible for filling the vacancy. Some may be reluctant to give you the salary range. If they balk, I suggest you say, "I need to know the salary range because I'm afraid I might be overqualified for the position." They'll usually give it to you when you explain this.

Let's suppose you haven't learned the salary range before an interview. The recruiter asks you: "What are your salary expectations?" You're earning $22,000 in your present position, but you know there are more responsibilities in the new position. You say that your salary expectations are $25,000. You feel you'll be happy with a $3,000 a year raise.

You're way off base in this case! If you had done your homework, you might have found that the salary range for this position (normally filled by a male) was $30,000 to $35,000. You goofed! Of course they're going to hire you for $25,000! But you'll be grossly underpaid for what you'll be doing — from the start of your employment and thereafter.

Now let's assume you did your homework in advance and learned that the salary range was $30,000-$35,000. What should you have told them your salary expectations were? Would you say $30,000 (as most women would)? Or $33,000 (as most men would)? I suggest you ask for $33,000. They're bound to negotiate with you, and you'll probably settle on about $31,500 as your starting salary. That's $6,500 per year more, or $542 more a month than the $25,000 you were originally willing to take! Quite a difference!

It doesn't end here, either. The woman who accepted the $25,000 starting salary would probably qualify for a cost-of-living increase after a year with the company. Let's say it's five percent. This would bring her salary up to $26,250. The second year's increase is the same, so her salary would go up to $27,562. If, however, she had obtained $31,500 originally, after a year she would be making $33,075 and after two years, $34,728. This would be $7,166 more! The gap is increasing between what she should have been getting and what she agreed to accept. And this gap will get larger and larger, unless she negotiates properly at the beginning of her employment.

If the recruiter asks what she was earning in her last position, she should explain that she was underpaid for the duties of her position, so it isn't relevant to the present position she's applying for (unless it's close to the salary range they're offering).

Initially, you may find it difficult to negotiate this way, but you have to feel you're worth it. Employers wouldn't assign salary ranges to these positions in the first place if they weren't worth this dollar amount.

WRITTEN JOB OFFERS

Don't accept an oral offer of a position and give notice to your present firm without a written job offer from the new company. The new company can back out, leaving you without a job. A written job offer is equivalent to a contract in a court of law. Most companies mail confirmation letters to their new employees spelling out the salary and benefits they have agreed on. This letter should confirm:

1. the salary agreed upon when the oral offer was accepted;
2. the title of the position you will hold;
3. the starting date and hours of employment;
4. the name and title of the person you report to and where and when you report;
5. the type and amount of relocation assistance (if required);
6. the length of the probationary period; if any.

It may also spell out the date of your first salary increase.

Make sure the letter states the length of your probationary period. One year is a long time and you'll be in an uncertain position until it's over. An employer can terminate an unacceptable employee at any time during the probationary period without having to go through formal disciplinary procedures (although the employer still has to document why the employee was unsuitable). As well, some benefits may not be given to new employees until their probationary period is over. If at all possible, try to get a three-month probationary period with a promise of a salary review at that time. After all, you won't be the novice you were when the company hired you three months earlier. You'll have learned the duties of the job and be more efficient in handling your duties, so you'll deserve more pay.

LESS WORK — MORE PAY

In the secretarial field, a junior secretary who works extremely hard from morning until night and often for more than one boss is paid peanuts. Executive secretaries are paid much more. (Of course, their responsibility level is higher.) If you wish to stay in the secretarial field, great — but why not work at the top instead of the bottom?

Employees who are paid by the hour (except those in the trades) receive the lowest salaries; employees paid by the week are next, followed by employees paid monthly. Managers' salaries are usually quoted in annual terms. If you know this, you can judge from an advertisement where you would fit into the corporate structure when it comes to discussing salary at the end of an interview. Note, too, that if your future boss doesn't interview you for your new job, the job isn't important; and that if routine, repetitive work takes up eighty to ninety percent of your job, it's probably a dead-end position.

SELLING YOURSELF IN AN INTERVIEW

To obtain a position, explain what *you* can do for a company (not what *they* can do for you)! Define your unique qualities. For instance, if you were applying for a supervisory position, you would give all the qualities you possess that make you a good supervisor.

Here are a few more tips to remember when applying for a position:

1. Learn whether a chronological résumé (experience listed in date order starting with most recent position) or a functional résumé (listing your transferable skills) or a portfolio (showing examples of your work) would work best. I use a chronological résumé when I'm asked by a company to do personnel work for them. If I'm asked to conduct training seminars, I use a functional résumé. On a first interview with a potential client for training, I also take my portfolio.

2. Get as much information as possible about a position before you go to the interview. Go to the library to check directories and the company's annual report. Learn how large the company is, what products it manufactures, or what services it provides. Check your local newspapers to see if they have a clipping file about the company. You'll be able to learn about

current and future projects the company is pursuing. Have a written list of questions, relating to this research, to ask during the interview.

INTERVIEW TIPS

1. Be on time for the interview — in fact be early, so you can check your appearance and review your information regarding the company and the position.

2. Let *them* interview *you.* You'll usually have time near the end of the interview to ask questions. Make sure you have several job-related questions ready.

3. Don't be put off by panel interviews (more than one person). There are several advantages to panel interviews.
   - There is less potential for bias or prejudice.
   - The supervisor, if present, usually has more specific information about the job itself (your co-workers, the number of staff in the area, the nature of the job itself).
   - Normally there's a representative from the human resources department. This person explains company benefits, pension plan, etc., knows how to keep others at the interview on track, and will stop illegal questions from being asked by others on the panel.
   - The third person may be the supervisor's supervisor, or possibly another supervisor (if there's more than one vacancy).

4. When you arrive for the interview, ask the receptionist for the name(s) of the interviewer(s). Repeat the name(s) until you know them by heart. When you're taken into the interview room, *you* should offer your hand for a handshake. Make sure you know how to shake hands properly. No wishy-washy handshakes. If you have problems in this area, practice until you're comfortable.

5. In the interview, don't be afraid to "toot your own horn." No one else is likely to do it for you. But don't lie! Talk loudly enough for them to hear you easily, but if you're nervous watch that the level of your voice doesn't rise.

6. Give concise, clear answers and try to avoid rambling. Keep all answers job-related. If you happen to have forgotten the question, don't be ashamed to say so; they know you're nervous and won't be turned off by this.

7. Never bad-mouth a former employer or company. This only makes *you* look bad — it just isn't done by successful people.
8. Know how to deal with illegal interview questions. To learn about illegal questions, contact your human rights commission and find out what these questions are. In Alberta, for example, questions relating to the private life of the person aren't allowed, either on the application form or during the interview.

ILLEGAL INTERVIEW QUESTIONS

Here are some sample interview questions that cannot be asked in Alberta and Manitoba. (These may not be the same in your province):

1. What church do you attend? In Alberta, they're allowed to ask what you do with your spare time or what organizations you belong to. In Manitoba, they may ask if you are willing to work shifts or a required work schedule. After you are hired they may ask about your religion to determine when leave of absence might be required for religious observances.
2. What does your spouse do? Where does he or she work?
3. How many children do you have? How old are they? What are their names and ages? How are they cared for?
4. What would your spouse think of your working overtime?
5. What would your spouse think of your having to travel with your job or stay overnight in some other city?
6. How old are you? What's your birth date? (They're allowed to ask questions related to age restrictions for licencing purposes only.)
7. I see you're married. What are your plans for having a family? Are you pregnant? When was your last period?
8. This job is usually a field that only men go into. What problems do you foresee?
9. Have you had any sexual harassment in any of your past jobs?
10. I see you've had to leave your past positions because your spouse was transferred. Do you anticipate that this will happen again in the near future?
11. Where were you born? Where are your ancestors from?
12. Do you have any physical disabilities? (This may only be asked if the job requires heavy lifting or other physical abilities. They may, however, make the job offer conditional on your passing a job-related physical or medical examination.)

Illegal Questions on Application Forms

1. Mr., Mrs., Miss, Ms, or male, female (This is optional in Manitoba.)
2. Height and weight (Alberta); hair and eye colour (Alberta and Manitoba.)
3. Request for a recent photograph
4. Race or colour
5. Religious affiliation
6. Birthplace, place of origin, ancestry or citizenship, status of parents, grandparents ("Are you legally permitted to work in this country?" is allowed.)
7. Christian name, maiden name ("Name used in previous employment and/or education?" is allowed, for purposes of checking references.)
8. Languages (Allowed if fluency in a language is required by the job.)
9. Date of birth ("Have you reached the age of majority?" or questions relating to licencing regulations are allowed.)

Questions Women are Often Asked in Interviews

The following describes illegal questions that women are often asked in interviews. To make it easier for you to deal with these questions, it's important for you to estimate why the interviewer is asking the question and what she or he really wants to know.

TYPE OF INTERVIEW QUESTIONS	WHAT THEY REALLY WANT TO KNOW
Are you married (planning to marry)? Are you thinking of starting a family soon?	What are your career plans for the next five years?
Do you have any children?	What does your work record look like in terms of absences, lateness, etc.
What does your husband do? Is he likely to be transferred soon?	Would you be willing to relocate?
Do you have little ones at home?	Can you work overtime? Would you be willing to travel?

Why do you work? (Doesn't your husband make enough?)

What salary do you expect?

Have you ever supervised men before? Do you have problems getting along with male colleagues at work?

Describe your supervisory style. How would you handle a subordinate who . . .?

Are you able to do strenuous physical work?

Have you been able to, in your past experience?

Would you get upset if . . .?

How do you handle stress? What would you do if . . .?

Are you capable of making fact-based decisions?

Describe your decision-making style.

Let's look at the first question in more detail: "Are you married? Are you thinking of starting a family soon?"

Most women would just like to reply, "Do you realize that that question is illegal?"

You can imagine how potential employers would react! *It would be better if you asked yourself* what they *really want to know*. In this case it's, "What are your career plans for the next five years?" When you've made this mental translation, your answer could be: "I assume you're wanting to know my career plans. I intend to devote the next ten years of my life to my career."

Do this with all the illegal questions that are thrown your way. It still won't prevent them from asking them, but at least you'll be able to live with the answers you give. Many women come away from an interview feeling soiled because they've answered these illegal questions and felt terrible that they allowed themselves to be subjected to harassment by a potential employer. With such high unemployment, many are reluctant to antagonize a possible employer. However, if you feel the need to object more strongly, you can lodge a complaint with your local human rights commission.

TRICKY INTERVIEW QUESTIONS
Interviewers may also ask such tricky questions as:
– Why do you think you would like to work for this company?

- Why should I hire *you* for this position?
- What are your strengths/weaknesses?
- Tell me about yourself.

Prepare before an interview and decide how to reply to these questions. Know reasons why you would like to work for the company. Tell them why you're well qualified for the position.

The question "What are your strengths?" often causes candidates to dry up. Be prepared for it. Have at least three or four things you feel you can do better than most people. Try it now. Write down what you think your strengths are. If you're having problems, ask a friend or family member to help you. For example:

- I'm extremely good at organizing things (give examples of complex things you've organized).
- I have very good interpersonal skills (give examples).
- I have the ability to motivate people beyond their normal level of production.
- I'm a high achiever and have high expectations of myself and my staff. (But be aware that the latter could be seen as a weakness — expecting too much of your staff.)
- I'm a self-starter and I work well without supervision.

These are the kinds of things employers want to hear. They don't care that you're a good swimmer or good at sports or a good mother. It's job-related strengths they want to learn about.

Be willing to discuss your weaknesses too. Can you identify your weaknesses? Take time to write these down right now. Many women have a tough time with this one, especially those who've never applied for a senior position. Often you can use your weaknesses to your advantage. For instance, when you investigated the position, you may have found that the company wanted someone who worked well without supervision, and who could handle numerous crisis situations without problems. You could explain that one of your weaknesses is that you have problems dealing with red tape. What does that tell people? That you're capable of making a lot of very quick decisions based on the information at hand. In essence, what you do is turn around what could be considered a negative trait and make it sound positive.

Another approach that often works is to explain that you're not very well organized but you're correcting the problem by attending time-management classes and using daytimers and "to do" lists. As well, outline other things you're doing to be better organized in the future. Whatever your failings are, describe what you're doing to correct them, or just don't mention them at all!

"Tell me about yourself." How are you likely to answer this question? As with the "strengths/weaknesses" question, you should use this opportunity to identify your good points. Don't miss this opportunity to sell yourself!

Interviews for senior positions differ from those for clerical or support-staff positions. In senior positions, you'll most likely work under pressure, interview others, and have to be a good decision maker, so they're likely to throw much more complex questions at you. There will probably be more than one person interviewing you and it may appear to be more of a grilling session — with you in the hot seat. You have to be ready for this experience. Just know your facts, and don't let them rattle you. If you do find yourself getting rattled, take a deep breath and make a conscious effort to answer their questions calmly and clearly. Slow down your speech and, if necessary, raise or lower the level of your voice. They'll be more likely to listen to what you have to say.

If they ask you a question you can't answer, admit it. If they throw one at you about a situation you've never encountered, say, "I've never been in that situation before. Give me a minute to think this one over . . . I would . . ." Let your intuition give you your best answer (believe in it — don't try to second-guess yourself).

What do you do if they won't let you finish your statement, but go on to the next question before you're finished? I'd suggest you say, "Before I answer this question, I'd like to finish answering the last one." Give the answer to the first question, then handle the second one. By this time you may have forgotten the second question, and you may have to ask them to repeat it. By following this strategy, you make them give you an opportunity to answer *all* of their questions. You're taking control of the situation, and they're thinking, "Hey, she knows how to do this — we can't rattle her!"

OVERTIME
Another thing that should be clarified in an interview is overtime requirements. It's assumed that people working in a subordinate position stay late — it's expected of them. This topic will be covered more in Chapter 7.

ACTING POSITIONS

When your boss goes away and puts you in charge of his or her job, this is called an acting position. There should be some monetary compensation because you will be handling your job and theirs at the same time. Before accepting this kind of assignment, ask if you will be paid more for this. It's better to know before giving your decision. If they say no, ask why. You might decide that you want and need this kind of experience because it will look good on your résumé. Being able to say that you worked as an acting supervisor might be something you want. So you have to judge for yourself whether you will insist on being paid more.

ASKING FOR A RAISE

Can you remember a time in your past when you asked for a raise? Many women have *never* asked for a raise. They assume that if they do they're being "pushy." They believe management sees this as a negative trait.

If you did ask for a raise, were you successful? I'll bet most of you were, simply because you had the initiative to ask. Men do it automatically. Women often think the company will "get mad at them" and they might get fired. This isn't what happens. The worst that will happen is that you'll be told no. If a man can say, "It's been fifteen months and I haven't received a raise. It's time, don't you think?", so can you.

However, this is the sort of thing you should try to find out when you're hired; it shouldn't have to be guesswork after you've taken the job. In the interview, ask what kind of salary increases you can expect and if the company has salary reviews on a regular basis. Determine if it has performance appraisals, and if so, how often they're done. Ask whether merit (or cost-of-living) increases coincide with the performance appraisal.

Do they have merit increases as well as cost-of-living increases? Don't always assume that if your company gives a five percent cost-of-living increase you're going to get five percent. Most employees don't realize that one employee might get two percent and another eight percent, depending on individual performance. These raises are often tied into a merit system. So if you get a two percent raise, what they're telling you is that you weren't giving them even average performance, that your work is determined to be below average. If you feel this isn't true, fight their decision with facts. Tell them why you think you were at least average, or possibly higher. (Unionized workers are an exception to these rules; their raises are more structured.)

Let's say it's getting close to the end of your probation period (June 1). Don't wait until June 1 to do something. Instead, on May 15 remind your boss that your probationary period will be up on June 1. Then on May 31, ask your boss what time she or he can see you on June 1 to discuss your salary increase. Some bosses still believe that if you don't ask for a raise, the money isn't important to you.

In your negotiations, avoid issuing the ultimatum that you'll quit if you don't get a raise. They just might take you up on it! Instead, document extra projects you've been doing since your last raise and bring these to your boss's attention. Prove you're worth a raise! If they don't give you one, you deserve to know why.

If you're working for a boss who has suddenly become successful, make sure you go in and ask for a raise, especially if you're in a secretarial or support position. If your boss gets a raise, so should you, because guess who helped him or her get there? Also, if your boss has taken on more responsibility, your job classification will likely change because your responsibilities will also be greater.

Unfortunately some bosses don't take you along with them when they receive a promotion. You might have to remind your boss that you were part of his or her success, and that you're ready for the new support position that goes along with his or her promotion. Try it — you've nothing to lose.

CHAPTER SEVEN

HOW TO HANDLE BEING OVERLOOKED FOR A PROMOTION AND OTHER WORK-RELATED PROBLEMS

Have you ever been overlooked for a promotion? Possibly you didn't even know the job was available, and someone else was hired? That's hard to take and very annoying. Here are some steps you can take to stop this from happening in the future.

The most important thing to remember when involving yourself in any kind of negotiation or confrontation with management is to keep your "cool"! Many women cry when they become angry. Do everything you can to avoid this. Try rehearsing the situation until it's no longer an emotional issue with you. Learn not to raise your voice, which is another thing women tend to do when they get angry. This is very grating on the ears of listeners. It also tells your employer that you've lost control of your side of the negotiations and helps him or her keep the upper hand. However, if you remain calm while you state your case (which you have supported with facts) you will win respect. You may find that this was all that was necessary — to state your case using facts, not emotions.

Try to guard against being overlooked for a promotion in future by making sure your boss knows what kind of career plans you have. Ask him or her to watch for any promotional opportunity that might help you get where you want to go. Otherwise, no matter how good your qualifications, you might be overlooked again. The oversight may be unintentional, the result of a certain type of conditioning. You have to make sure your employer recognizes that you're a candidate for promotion. You might also talk to people in the human resources department. Explain that you're looking for a promotional opportunity and ask to be kept informed about any that come up.

It's also a good idea to ask your supervisor what he or she feels is missing in your training or background that might be keeping you from being promoted. A boss who is on your side can be a great ally because he or she will be expending time and effort to help you get where you want to be. So be open about your goals. Ask your supervisor to help you obtain training or experience and to recommend you for promotions he or she thinks fit your qualifications.

Consider another type of situation. There's a promotional position in your company that you've applied for because you believe you're well qualified for it. You submit your résumé for consideration and learn that someone else has been hired for the position. You *know* this person is less qualified than you and you're upset. What steps should you take? How should you approach this situation? Is it too late to do something about it? No, it isn't. But simply complaining to the hiring supervisor, or saying "How come you hired somebody who's less qualified than I?" is unlikely to work.

I suggest you phone the supervisor who was in charge of hiring and ask for fifteen minutes of his time (we'll assume that it's a man). If he asks why, explain that it's important for you to obtain some information regarding the position. He'll have his guard up, but if you're persistent he'll see you. He expects you to attack him and will be on the defensive, even before you enter the room. So your approach has to be gentle. (The hard-nosed approach of most labour negotiations won't work in this situation.)

You may object to this softer approach and feel that pussyfooting around someone who has been unfair is impossible. However, in my experience, the approach I suggest works much better than a direct, angry confrontation. You accomplish the same end, but nobody gets irate.

You could start by being honest and admitting you're upset. Say, "I think you know I was really looking forward to being accepted for this position, and it has upset me that I wasn't chosen. Can you help me determine what I'm missing in my background that's keeping me from being promoted?"

He'll feel he's somewhat off the hook because you're discussing your failings, not questioning the decision. If he says, "The other person was just better qualified than you," your response should be, "Could you be more specific about the qualifications that are necessary for the job?" After he has pointed out the qualifications, paraphrase what he has said, then add, "I have that kind of experience — in fact, I have more than you've said is necessary for that position, so I guess that isn't the problem."

He'll have to admit you're right. "No, I guess not. You have seven years' experience in that area." (You know that George, who got the job, has only five years' experience. Don't throw this at the supervisor — store this information for later.)

Next you ask, "What *other* kinds of qualifications were necessary for this position?"

He may suggest some additional type of knowledge or experience, and your reply might be: "I don't think that's a problem either." Here you would give further facts showing that you have these qualifications as well (assuming you do). In short, keep giving factual reasons why you don't think his explanation eliminates you as a candidate. He'll try to pull out some plausible reason why you didn't get the job, and he won't be able to do it.

At the end of the interview, you say something like, "Well, I don't know where this leaves me, because it appears that, from what you've just told me, I was the best qualified for the job. As you stated, as far as experience is concerned, I needed five years' experience, and I have seven. I know George only has five. As far as education goes, I have . . . and I know George has only . . . I'm still at a loss to know why he got the job and I didn't. What do we do now?"

You've put this person on the spot. You've presented your facts in such a way that it can't be denied that you're right.

Many would say that all you've done is make the person angry. This may be so, but the supervisor will be angry because you're right and he's wrong. This may be the time to ask for an impartial person to be involved. If you're in a union environment, your steward could be called in to mediate. If it's a non-union environment, a representative of the human resources department could be called in to solve the dilemma.

Another choice could be to mark time and leave the meeting with this comment; "Well, it's unfortunate that this happened. I really feel upset, because I should have been given the job. Can I count on you to see that I won't be overlooked for the next promotion?"

This type of approach is low-key without being wishy-washy. You keep your cool — and your temper — but also give yourself a better chance of being treated fairly in the future. It might put the company in a very difficult position to demand that they pull back the promotion they have already offered to George. If George had been given a written job offer, he would be able to sue the company. You may have let the company off the hook. They may even recommend you for a promotion in another department. In fact, that's one of the things you can ask them to do.

Would you feel comfortable doing it this way? I hope so. It's a win/win situation. If you want to take a stab at it, there are many things you can do to prepare for this kind of confrontational meeting. I suggest you rehearse the meeting with a close friend. Try to ensure that your friend is a good negotiator who can play "the boss" well. This person should confront you with difficult things that are relevant to the situation you're going to face — every roadblock the boss is likely to throw at you. Practise until you can respond not with anger or tears but as if you're acting a part; learn to pull yourself mentally away from the situation. If possible, pretend you're negotiating on behalf of another person. You'll become less emotionally involved. Have you tried this technique before?

If a friend isn't available, try using a tape recorder. Rehearse what you're going to say over and over until it becomes automatic. Use this technique whenever you have to face a difficult encounter.

You might conclude that this approach isn't for you. It depends how strongly you feel about the situation. You may say to yourself, "I don't give a hoot about this company. I'm going to fight this; a principle is at stake here. I'm not going to sit idly by and let someone else take the position that should be mine!" and decide to take the issue to the top. Your first step should be to contact your company personnel department. If your company's too small to have one, speak to a senior official. If he or she doesn't help, lodge a complaint with the human rights commission.

Many people assume that because they've filled an acting position, they're automatically going to be promoted into that position when it becomes available. Wrong. Companies may hire someone off the street. You may feel like asking the person in charge why you're good enough to work in an acting capacity, but not good enough to handle the job now that it's open. Before complaining, check the prerequisites of the job. Is it possible that you're missing important education or training? If so, ask your boss to help you obtain this training. If you *are* qualified, back up your statements with facts about why you should have been hired.

PROMOTIONS IN BANKING

Many companies are changing their philosophy toward female employees. Twenty years ago it was likely that the only job you thought of when considering working for a bank was that of a teller or secretary. Things have changed. According to the Canadian Bankers' Association, seventy percent of the supervisory positions — jobs paying more than $20,000 — within banks today are held by women. Unfortunately, however, there were only fifteen female vice-presidents and fourteen female directors of Canadian banks in July 1986. Table 7:1, supplied by the Canadian Bankers' Association, gives the details.

TABLE 7:1
Women as a Percentage of Full-time Employees
by Organization/Salary Level
Canadian Chartered Banks 1975, 1984, and 1986

Organization Level	Salary Level**	Women - Number & Percentage of full-time employees*					
		1975		1984		1986	
		Number	%	Number	%	Number	%
Senior Management	$66+	4	0.2	28	1.4	46	2.4
Middle Management	$36-66	469	4.1	3,410	16.6	3,542	17.7
Junior Management/ Supervisory	$22-36	23,530	57.5	30,876	71.1	26,289	69.4
Administrative/ Support	<$22	63,854	93.3	65,693	93.5	66,443	92.5
Management	$29+	6,805	22.0	10,957	30.1	10,260	29.4
Management/ Supervisory	$22+	24,003	44.3	34,314	52.1	29,877	50.0
ALL LEVELS		87,857	71.7	100,008	73.4	96,320	73.2

* In Canada   ** Expressed in 1986 terms   < Less than

Management appears to be changing its views about where women belong in business. For instance, according to J.K. Johnston, director of human resources of Great-West Life Assurance Co., "Ten years ago, a non-management, non-clerical, secretarial group of staff constituting approximately 60% of the total Head Office population was split approximately 75%/25% male to female. Today, it is the exact opposite. Advancement in our company is truly based on one's own ability . . . We provide an atmosphere which promotes self-development and every staff member is entitled to take advantage [of it]."

FREEDOM FROM THE PINK-COLLAR GHETTO

Here are some suggestions that may help you move up from a pink-collar position.

Step 1. Go through the goal-setting process. Decide *where* you want to go. Then investigate *how* you can get there. Is it through on-the-job training, or will you require formal education and/or training? Once you find out, get that training, possibly while working at a junior-level position in the field of your choice.

Step 2. Document every task you do in your present position. Determine whether you're doing an important part of your boss's job. Look for those tasks that require independent action and/or decision making on your part. You'll find that if you can identify the decisions you now make, you may be able to convince your employer that you're capable of making more major ones. You'll just be using different kinds of data. Look for duties in which your judgment was crucial to the outcome of a task. Look for clear-cut areas of responsibility, authority and accountability. In other words, look for things you do on a regular basis in which *you* decide on the outcome. These are the skills management requires, and you'll be well paid for using them.

Step 3. Ask your boss if your talents could be utilized in other areas of his or her department. Explain that you're willing to take a cut in salary. (Even a junior position, as long as it has a toehold on the bottom rung of the promotional ladder, is better than a clerical or secretarial one.) If your boss doesn't think this is a good idea, talk to the human resources department. Identify the decision-making qualities you've developed and what specialty you would like to get into. Ask personnel to let you know about any positions that come up that would utilize your qualifications.

As a backup, watch for job postings on the company bulletin board, and be sure to apply for positions you believe you can handle. Have the human resources department explain why you're not suitable for the vacancies you're rejected for. This may be hard at first, but they'll explain where you need to improve your qualifications.

Step 4. Talk with someone in a high position who's eager to see women progress in business, and ask his or her advice on what kinds of experience or education you're lacking.

Step 5. When responding to ads, stay clear of those that describe the position or the candidate with words such as "skills," "right arm," "high-class," "bright," "achiever," "hard working," "support services," "assistant to," "pleasant working conditions," etc. These denote lower-level positions.

Watch instead for words such as "self-starter," "career-oriented," "challenging position," etc.

Step 6. Ask senior women in the company to help you reach your goal. Most of them will be glad to help you. Ask them how they got where they are and the route they took to get there.

OTHER WORK PROBLEMS

The "Leap-frog" Syndrome

Have you ever trained someone and then watched that person get the promotion instead of you? Follow the same advice I gave earlier in this chapter, and approach your boss about it. If your employer favours your male co-workers for retraining or promotional opportunities, you might have to go so far as to complain to the human rights commission. But if you can't prove sex-based discrimination or you prefer not to complain formally, there are several more informal but effective options you can try.

– Organize a status-of-women committee with your female co-workers to approach your employer with positive suggestions for the retraining and promotion of women.

– Let the human resources department know about your interest in existing employee-training programs and/or suggest new ones to them.

– Check out local adult-education courses to expand your own horizons. (You may have to pay for this yourself.)

– Ask your local employment centre about free government retraining programs that may be available.

The Dead-end Job

At one of my seminars a participant asked: "How do I handle a situation where I started a job in a department where there was plenty to learn (that's why I took the job), but no one will let me learn more? My job duties are done long before the day's over, so I've asked for more responsibility and have even asked co-workers for some of their work. My boss has objected, and my co-workers are a little cool with me."

I suggested that if she is given a higher level of responsibility in her position, she'll also be placed in a higher job classification, which will put her into a higher pay range. Her boss knows this'll happen. And if she attempts to do some of the tasks of her co-workers, they might assume that she's trying to take over their jobs. This could be very threatening to them. It sounded to me as if she was hired into a position for which she was overqualified in the first place, and that the position offered little room for growth and development of her abilities. Her best course of action is to apply for more senior positions.

Foot-dragging Co-workers

Another participant, Margaret, said her co-workers didn't seem to know how to deal with deadlines; they extended them all the time. She explained that when they were wasting time she got mad and would tell them to work harder. I asked her if she supervised them, and she admitted they were co-workers rather than her subordinates. I explained to her that she was acting out the role of a supervisor (without the authority) in criticizing her co-workers' work. Naturally they objected and were probably thinking, "Who does she think she is?" She was responsible for only her own work, not that of her co-workers. The person responsible for the performance of her co-workers is the supervisor. Her best course is to back off and make sure she does her own work properly.

Another participant, Della, inquired, "I feel I'm doing far more work than my two co-workers who waste a lot of time taking personal calls and talking to each other."

The supervisor's help is needed here. I suggested that Della offer to gather details. For instance, let's say there's a pool of work that she and two other employees do as time permits. She should try to determine some measuring tool that would show how much each employee does. She could possibly determine this by counting the files processed each day. She might find that thirty files are processed in a normal day. She should then determine who handled each file. It wouldn't take long for the supervisor to recognize that the two co-workers are averaging eight files each a day and Della is averaging twelve. The supervisor must then determine whether the work is being done accurately. If all accuracy rates are the same, there's no problem. But if the one doing the most files (Della) is making more mistakes, she should be encouraged to slow down and do fewer files.

Let's assume, though, that the accuracy rate is the same for all three workers. The supervisor could call the three workers into her office. She would give them the information she's gathered regarding the total number of files completed in the department and explain that from now on each employee will be delegated ten files each per day to process. End of problem. Della does not need to accuse the two slower workers of not doing their share. With her supervisor's help, they now know what's expected of them. This, of course, takes a supervisor who is fair and just. Analyse your supervisor — would he or she go along with this?

Dumping or "Job Enlargement"

Marcie's problem was that most of her duties were under that catch-all phrase "other duties as assigned." If more than ten percent of your duties fit into this category, your job description isn't accurate. Get it updated. If your company is using an official job-classification system, they know this is the percentage allowed under that category.

Marcie's next problem was how to reply when her supervisor started every new task with the statement: "It's a marvellous opportunity. How can you refuse an opportunity that might get you ahead?"

If these opportunities really will teach you something you wouldn't learn any other way and that you need for your next step up, you should grab them. Keep in mind that this person is actually teaching you how to do his or her job. As far as development goes, it's to your advantage to accept. When you are interviewed for your next promotion, you'll be able to say: "I was given this project to do by my boss, and I handled it well." You'll be able to prove you're capable of doing the duties of the more demanding position.

But what if that "opportunity" is really just an addition to your workload that makes it harder for you to stay on top of your work?

If they're really dumping on you, then we're getting into what's called "job enlargement." This term means that they're giving you more of the same level of tasks. This often happens when companies cut staff. Four people are often doing the work that five used to do. Effective time management should eliminate this and keep you on top of what you're really capable of doing.

On the other hand, "job enrichment" (also called "development") means there'll be opportunities to learn new things that will most likely help you towards your next promotion.

Barbara's problem was similar. She kept having tasks added to her position without having any change in the level of position she was filling. This was either a job-description problem or (if she was being given more of the same) a job-dumping problem.

If these new responsibilities were becoming a regular part of her job, I suggested she should ask for her job description to be updated, first making sure she had the facts to show her boss how the level of responsibility of tasks had changed.

Overtime Overload

Another participant said: "We don't get paid overtime no matter how many hours we work!"

In Alberta, the employer may either pay employees time and a half for overtime or give them time off in lieu of overtime pay (the employee must sign an agreement for the latter to be given). By law, overtime pay is given for anything more than eight hours a day, or forty-four hours a week. I urged her to check the labour laws where she lives regarding overtime. If you don't know the law, find out. It's usually a department or ministry of labour that looks after this.

Betty had a slightly different problem. Her boss made her feel as if she was inadequate because she didn't handle the job the same way her predecessor had done. It turned out that the other woman had voluntarily worked until eight o'clock every night without extra pay.

Don't fall for that one! I suggested she talk to her boss and say, "When I took this position I was told that the hours of work were eight to four, and that there *might* be some overtime. I find that to get my work done, I have to work overtime almost every night.

This isn't what I was led to expect. Am I expected to work overtime every night without extra pay?"

How do you convince them that they need extra staff? Use facts. The facts are that you've had to work overtime almost every night to take care of rush jobs (*supply time sheets to prove this*). Work given to you by departments is getting out later and later every week (*give details*). You're hearing verbal complaints from people who have had to wait too long for their work (*give details*). Reports are late (*name which ones*), morale is down (*give examples*), and mistakes are being made because you have to rush (*give details*). Remember, your boss has to justify to his or her supervisors why that department needs extra staff, so give him or her the ammunition needed to accomplish this. Don't keep attempting to cope and cope — you'll just get further under.

Or the following solution to the problem (based on the fact that businesses want to save money) could be suggested. After giving your employer a copy of the overtime agreement and discussing it with him or her, you could say: "I suggest that you get someone in to look after my overload work. You'll be paying me time and a half for overtime, and by that time of the day I'm tired and can't give you my best work. On the other hand, if you hired a part-time employee, this person would be paid regular wages and would come to the work fresh. This person could probably handle some of Sally's work, too, because she and I are often the only ones here at that time of the night. Between Sally and me, I'm sure there's enough work to have the person come in three to four hours a day. What do you think of this?"

Janet also had an overtime problem. "I had to start mentioning on Monday that they shouldn't expect me to work late Thursday night because I had made other plans. Otherwise they would have expected me to be on call. I find I can't make plans any more." She should have a meeting with her boss to clarify when she is expected to work late.

The Disorganized Boss

Tanya voiced another common problem: "My boss is disorganized and doesn't appear to know what's going on. I'm very organized. What should I do?"

I suggested she ask him if there were any duties he would like to delegate to her that would lighten his load. Of if she were feeling brave, she could ask him if he would like her to help him become more organized. If this is impossible, she has two choices. She can relax and tolerate the chaos or ask for a transfer to another position.

Too Many Bosses

Margie had problems dealing with more than one boss. Quite often she had two top-priority things to do at the same time, for two different people. I suggested she talk to the two supervisors, explain her dilemma and ask *them* to make the decision. She shouldn't have to make it herself, unless they were absent and couldn't give their input.

Grace also had this problem, with a twist. She asked if this tactic would work when one boss was more senior than the other. Again, if the senior one gave her a new job, she should say, "Bill asked me to do this job. Does your task take precedence over that one?" Let *him* make the decision.

Job-classification Inequities

Margaret asked, "What if a female and male are doing essentially the same job, and the male's being paid more. What can the woman do?" She had already confronted her manager and asked why this had happened. She had sent in her job description and it had come back unchanged, still in a lower classification than her male co-worker.

I suggested she ask for a personal interview, take to the interview *all* the facts and written documentation to back up her claim, and show her boss the indisputable evidence that the two positions had the same level of responsibility. She has the right as an employee to fight for this equality. It's important for all workers to compare their jobs with those of others in the same department, especially if the staff is a mixture of men and women. In the past, women have been reluctant to do this. It's one of the main equal-rights and equal-opportunity issues facing government and businesses today.

However, an employee in this position should also be willing to listen to the employer's side of the story. There might be extenuating circumstances she isn't aware of. The other position may call for more experience or education than hers.

If you find you're underpaid and can't get your company to

change the situation, the human rights commission will fight for you to make sure both of you (male and female) are paid the same salary for the same level of work.

What if you are having difficulty seeing the job descriptions of your co-workers?

I don't understand why companies do this. It's important for employees to know the responsibilities of the workers around them, if they are to understand the company. If you can't get the description from your supervisor or manager, ask your co-workers themselves for copies of their job descriptions. Explain that you need the information as a guide for updating your own description. (You're not lying — if your job description was completed more than two years ago, it's probably outdated.) Say that yours isn't accurate, and you'd like to review an accurate one. Try it — it just might work.

You might also try talking to the people in the human resources department. They have copies of the job descriptions for all positions in the company and may be willing to release this information, even if your boss won't.

Many women fear they might be fired if they "make waves" and ask for an accurate job description even though they are entitled to it. But your employer wouldn't dare fire you either for requesting an up-to-date job description, or for pointing out that your job has been incorrectly classified. Make sure you document your struggle to obtain equality. In your place a man would almost certainly fight for an accurate description and classification.

If you are involved in updating your job description, use strong action verbs such as "responsible for, in charge of, in control of, supervises," etc.

THE IMPORTANCE OF FEEDBACK IN SOLVING PROBLEMS AT WORK

If you've been upset or aggravated by something someone has done and haven't really known what to do about the situation, learning how to use feedback may alleviate your problem.

Consider the problem one receptionist encountered. Her job required her to take messages for all the office staff. One particular client (Mr. Wilson) phoned in repeatedly asking to speak to Mr. Jordan. The messages were passed on promptly to Mr. Jordan.

However, when Mr. Wilson accused her one day of neglecting to pass on his messages to Mr. Jordan, she realized Mr. Jordan hadn't been returning Mr. Wilson's calls. She wondered how she would deal with this situation, as it was likely to happen again. What should she tell Mr. Wilson the next time he phoned?

She was trying to deal with the wrong problem. Her boss, Mr. Jordan, was the problem, not Mr. Wilson! I asked her if she had ever thought of explaining the problem she was encountering to her boss.

"Oh," she said. "I couldn't do that!"

I then asked, "How is the situation going to change unless he knows what his behaviour does to you? You're not even giving him the opportunity to fix the problem."

Feedback Procedure
The process of feedback works as follows:
1. You explain the problem or situation to the person causing the difficulty;
2. You define the feelings or reactions (anger, sadness, anxiety, etc.) his or her behaviour produces in you;
3. You suggest a solution. (IMPORTANT POINT: You may leave the solution up to the person causing the difficulty.)

In feedback, you share your reactions to another person's behaviour with that person. People can't attempt to change their behaviour unless you let them know what their actions are doing to you.

In the receptionist's case, I suggested she talk to her boss. Rather than saying what she really felt (which might be: "You turkey, you never return phone messages!"), she should say, "I have a problem and I need your help in solving it. Mr. Wilson has phoned in five times, and he's really annoyed at me because you haven't returned his calls. This upsets me. What do you suggest I tell him the next time he calls?"

To take another example: a co-worker — Bill — is often late for work. This makes your job twice as busy when you have to cover for him. You're pretty upset and want to discuss the issue with him. After thinking about how the feedback process works, you decide to say, "Bill, I don't think you realize the double workload I have every time you're late. I don't think this is fair to me, do you? What can be done about it?"

Here's how this worked:

1. The problem: you have a double workload when he's late for work.
2. Your feelings or reactions: it's not fair to you.
3. The solution: you ask *him* to provide one.

A final example: Margo, a co-worker, is always interrupting you with small talk, ruining your concentration. You're getting upset because this is putting you behind in your work. Rather than wait until you're ready to explode with, "For God's sake, shut up, Margo!" you say something like, "Margo, I'm working on an important project. I guess you don't realize it, but every time you interrupt me, I lose my train of thought. Can we talk later at coffee break?"

1. The problem: her interruptions.
2. The effect on you: you lose your train of thought.
3. The solution: you suggest talking later, at coffee break.

Many people stop unacceptable behaviour once you bring it to their attention. Others need further attention. If Margo did the same thing two hours later, what should you tell her? Repeat your original statement, because this may have become a habit with Margo and she may have done it without thinking.

The next morning, guess what? She's at it again. What should you do? Say, "Margo, twice yesterday I mentioned that I'm working on an important project and that your interruptions affect my concentration. Can you tell me why you're still doing this?" This makes Margo account for her aggressive actions. (Yes, she's being aggressive now, because she knows she's bothering you). Give consequences should her behaviour continue. Tell her you will have to report her to your supervisor if it happens again.

Another day goes by, and Margo is at it again. What should you do the fourth time? This is when you call in reinforcements and talk to your boss. I suggest you say, "I have a problem and I need your help in solving it. On Tuesday, I spoke to Margo and explained . . ." And you explain everything you have done to stop the behaviour. Then you ask, "What do you suggest I do next time she interrupts me?" Normally, your supervisor will talk to Margo because Margo is wasting company money, and as she reports to him or her, your supervisor is ultimately responsible for what Margo does. Will Margo like you? Do you care? She's going to cause you trouble whether you go to your boss or not.

To recap, here are the steps you take:
1. Follow the three steps in the feedback procedure.
2. If the behaviour happens again, repeat step one.
3. On the third occasion, make the person account for continuing to do something known to bother you.
4. On the fourth occasion, go to a higher authority.

Use the wording "I have a problem and I need your help in solving it," whenever someone is causing you grief — even if it is the person you're talking to. You're not shaking your finger at the person and bawling him or her out for unacceptable behaviour. And it will often produce the results you're after.

CHAPTER EIGHT

PROBLEMS OF FEMALE SUPERVISORS

Many women won't admit it, but they have sexist attitudes. They appear unable to take orders from female supervisors. Unconsciously, they feel that only men should be supervisors. As a result, they question the ability of their woman supervisors and make things difficult for them.

Have you ever reported to a female boss? Was she a good or bad supervisor? If she was inept as a supervisor, do you have any idea why? One of the major reasons why many women fail as supervisors is that they've never had any kind of supervisory training. These women are set up to fail by management, as is anyone put into a supervisory role without proper training.

It's extremely important for any woman climbing the corporate ladder to obtain adequate supervisory training, preferably *before* she takes her first supervisory position. If she's a supervisor now, she owes it to herself to get this training *whether her company pays for it or not*. People who don't know how to act as supervisors appear unsure of themselves. Others lose respect for them and take advantage of them. It's just not true that people are born knowing how to supervise.

Do you recall any situations in which you or your co-workers sabotaged your female boss? Did you make her look even worse than she was? Sometimes the temptation to do this is overwhelming; but before you give in to it, ask yourself, "What will I really be doing by making her look bad?" You will be making *all* female supervisors look bad.

When you're working for a woman boss, it's your responsibility to help her look good. Why? Because in most cases a woman who is promoted to a supervisory or management position is on trial. If she fails, this reflects on all the women who follow her. Every time you help a woman fail at her job, you hold back others who may be qualified — including perhaps yourself; if she doesn't make it, management is going to think twice before they hire another "dud," so without knowing it, you could be holding yourself back from promotional opportunities.

If you do everything in your power to make your female supervisor look good, she'll most likely pull you along with her (faster than most male bosses). Start by explaining to her you understand the pressure she's under and that you're on her side. Tell her you want her to succeed and will do everything you can to make her look good. For example, you may hear things from your peers that she'll never hear at her level, so you could keep her informed. Explain to her as well what your own career goals are, and ask her to let you know if there's a more responsible job available that she thinks you can handle. Let her know you want to prepare yourself for future promotions, and ask her to help you develop your abilities and improve your knowledge and experience.

Does any of this change your attitude toward female supervisors?

You should tell a male boss the same thing (but be aware that this is *not* one of the games played in business, so he might be a little confused by your offer. Still, it's worth trying. What have you got to lose?)

If *you're* a female boss and are having problems with your female subordinates, explain the situation to them. If you hear that someone is trying to sabotage you, be direct. Say, "I really need your support and your help, and I notice that you're not co-operating. I'd like to know why."

Janet had a problem that at one time was rare, but that crops up more often now that young women are becoming more educated and able to take on supervisory roles at an earlier age. A twenty-five-year-old college graduate, she was hired by a company to supervise its clerical division. She had four years' experience in an office but wasn't prepared to supervise women almost twice her age who had an average of ten to fifteen years' office experience. They were openly hostile to her and did everything *but* co-operate.

Janet decided to ask Sarah, one of the less-hostile women, into her office to discuss the problem. Sarah was honest. She admitted she had been surprised and disappointed when Janet had been "hired off the street" as her supervisor. She had pictured someone her own age or older filling the position — possibly one of her peer group, or someone whose experience she felt would give her the "right" to supervise. Instead, she found a woman the same age as her daughter in the role. She admitted that when Janet complimented her on a job well done she felt patronized, and that when she was disciplined she felt defensive. Once these feelings were brought out into the open, the two women were able to start over. Janet now understood the reasons for Sarah's antagonism and could deal with it better. Sarah understood why she felt as she did and made an effort to change her attitude toward Janet.

Soon Janet called a meeting with the rest of her staff to discuss the situation with them. She explained that she understood how they felt and told them what she expected from them and that she was counting on them to co-operate. She then asked each staff member, "Can I count on you in the future?" One employee, Julie, appeared reluctant to make a commitment to her, so Janet knew she would have to keep an eye on her. Soon the woman's low productivity and poor work made it necessary for Janet to discipline her. She again explained to Julie what she expected from her and what the consequences would be if Julie kept on producing sloppy work. Unfortunately, Julie never did accept Janet. She kept on producing sloppy work and eventually had to be fired.

Janet fared better with the others. When she noticed a decided change in attitude and productivity, she thanked them for their understanding and co-operation.

Traditionally, society has taught us that the older woman — the mother or the aunt — knows more, so therefore is to be treated with deference and respect. Switching roles is disconcerting to both the young female supervisor (who's suddenly in the position of the "mother"), and the older female employee (who's now in the position of the "daughter" seeking approval). These feelings are related to beliefs about power and who should have it. It's a situation with no set solutions that will work every time.

Support staff (mainly women) normally go out of their way to keep their bosses (usually male) organized, on time and comfortable. They nurture their bosses (bring them coffee, remind them of appointments, open and sort their mail). But when a woman is in the supervisory position, the nurturing may stop unless she's on top of the situation. She'll have to let her staff know she expects the same kind of service the former male supervisor received.

When correcting a subordinate's behaviour, she should concentrate on the work-related behaviour (e.g., sloppy reports) rather than on the subordinate's attitude. She'll also have to find ways to show she respects the experience and expertise of her subordinates. She should learn about the career goals of her subordinates and show them she's willing to help them reach their goals.

Barbara supervised a staff of three men. She was an engineer and the men were technologists. Her subordinates didn't seem to listen to her and insisted on doing things "their" way. Fortunately, before taking the position, she had taken steps to get proper supervisory training, which equipped her to act confidently. It became necessary to have a disciplinary interview with one of her male subordinates when he refused to do a task Barbara had assigned him. This was a case of insubordination (a very serious problem) that could have led to the termination of the employee. She handled it herself and placed a strong written warning on the employee's file stating that he would be terminated if it happened again. Later, to keep him up-to-date, she informed her supervisor and he commended her on the competent way she had handled the touchy situation. Could you have done this if you were supervising men? If you're planning to climb the ladder, it's a distinct possibility that you will be supervising men in the future. Make sure you're prepared to handle it.

CHAPTER NINE

HOW TO BE A GOOD SUPERVISOR

ESSENTIAL SUPERVISORY RESPONSIBILITIES

Has your company given you a supervisory title?

Many men and women are given the title of supervisor, but their companies don't give them the authority to carry out the duties of their positions effectively. They're really only "lead hands," with little or no control over their subordinates' actions. To determine if yours is a true supervisor's position, ask yourself if your job has the four essential characteristics of supervisory work. Are you responsible for:

1. delegating work to subordinates?
2. checking subordinates' work?
3. conducting performance appraisals?
4. disciplining subordinates?

The first two responsibilities are usually given to all people with the title "supervisor" or "foreman." However, the second two often aren't. A fifth responsibility would be that of hiring your own staff.

Let us look more closely at each of these in turn.

Delegating work to subordinates

These are the actual tasks you give to your subordinates for completion.

Checking subordinates' work

This is checking to see that tasks you've delegated have been completed properly. You'll check the quality and quantity of the work and how long it took to complete.

Conducting performance appraisals

You should be the one that does the performance appraisals for all your subordinates — nobody else. Your boss shouldn't do it because he or she isn't directly responsible for the work of your subordinates. Your supervisor might review your findings to see if they're fair, but *you* complete the appraisal on each and every employee you supervise.

Disciplining subordinates

Because ultimately your staff makes you look either good or bad, you need this control to correct production and/or behaviour problems.

Hiring your own staff

This is a plus and not always allowed by companies. Whenever possible, have as much input as you can into the hiring of the people who work for you. If you're on a different "wave length" from a subordinate, it can be very difficult for both you and the subordinate to work as a team.

How does your supervisory position measure up? If you don't have all of the first four, you're in very bad shape. You'll receive questionable respect from your subordinates and have little control over the outcome of their work.

For example: I delegated a task to a subordinate and, when I reviewed her work, found it unsatisfactory. I took her aside to explain my dissatisfaction with her performance. She replied, "So what? It looks good enough to me." If I hadn't had the authority to discipline her, I would have had no control over how she completed her work. Without the authority to say to her, "Unless your performance improves, I'm going to have to put a written disciplinary warning in your file," I would have been handicapped. With that authority, I could let her know that if she didn't perform, eventually out she'd go.

If you don't have this minimum amount of control over your employees and they do a lousy job, who looks bad? You! If this is the situation your company has put you in, you owe it to yourself to talk to your boss and insist that all four responsibilites (and the fifth if at all possible) are given to you.

If you've not been given the responsibility of conducting performance appraisals, discuss it with your boss: "I understand the main responsibilities of a supervisor are . . . and I find I'm missing one of them — that of actually preparing and conducting performance appraisals for my staff. How do you feel about this?" If you run into conflict, explain, "If I don't have this right, you've removed some of my control, and I need that control to do a good job."

Supervisory training is crucial for men and women who wish to succeed in business. It's the first step toward management training, which is much more intensive. It's important for you to realize that a supervisory role is very different from a non-supervisory one. Though not necessarily on the path to the top, you have an important function to perform. Unless you do your job well, your subordinates, the company, and most of all *you* will look bad.

Some participants in my intensive three-day supervisory training seminar have been in supervisory positions for years with no supervisory training at all. As a result they have had to learn the ropes by trial and error — they've been forced to "re-invent the wheel." How much easier it would have been for them if they had received training, either *before* commencing their supervisory responsibilities or shortly thereafter.

Look for supervisory training that covers the following topics:

The Role of the Supervisor
Being a supervisor is tough. Managers are above you telling you their expectations. Below you are your staff who can make you look either good or bad. You're expected to co-operate with other supervisors, be a mediator in union disputes, and implement policy with the help of other staff groups. You're caught in the middle, being pulled in every direction. Many foremen (another type of supervisor) have told me that they had no idea how their job responsibilities would change when they accepted a foreman's position.

There must be a distinct line between you and your subordinates, unless you're a "working supervisor." Supervisors are responsible for everything they and their subordinates do. If an employee puts in a sloppy report — it makes both employee *and* supervisor look bad. If employees do good work, the supervisor looks good too.

Leadership Styles

There are six basic leadership styles, ranging from authoritarian to participative.

1. *Supervisor makes the decision and announces it.* For instance, if there's a rule or regulation your company wishes you to impose, you'll have to lead with a Theory X method (authoritarian) by saying, "This is how it's going to be done." There's no flexibility in this approach.
2. *Supervisor "sells" the decision.* The supervisor explains why the rule or regulation is necessary.
3. *Supervisor presents ideas, invites questions.* The supervisor allows employees to ask questions about the new rule or regulation.
4. *Supervisor presents a tentative decision subject to change.* The supervisor is thinking of implementing a new rule or regulation and asks for input from employees.
5. *Supervisor presents the problem, gets suggestions, then makes the decision.* The supervisor still makes the final decision.
6. *Supervisor defines the limits and requests the group to make the decision.* The supervisor says to employees, "Here's a problem — you're on your own as to how you solve it. Let me know if you need help." This is a strong Theory Y method (participative).

In a supervisory training course, participants are encouraged to determine which of the six styles would be best to use in each leadership situation.

Delegation

This can be a tricky area for someone who has been taking orders most of his or her life. Most supervisors don't understand the delegation process. When you delegate a task to an employee, you can't divorce yourself from the task. You can't say, "I told Sally to do that and she didn't do it correctly." You're saying that Sally looks bad. Wrong. *You* look bad! (That's how employees can sabotage their bosses.) Your job as a supervisor is to get the best out of your employees, to challenge them, to develop their talents and see that they do the delegated tasks properly.

Also important is learning to give tasks to the right person at the right level, so your company spends its money well. For example: Many secretaries hate making coffee.

You, as her supervisor, may empathize, and decide that you'll take your turn at making coffee. Your manager sees this and questions you about it: "I saw you making coffee the other day — how come?" You explain: "The secretaries really don't want to get stuck with that chore all the time, so I do my share of coffee making." The manager says, "Look, I pay you twenty-five dollars an hour. You shouldn't be spending valuable time making coffee."

When you see this issue from management's point of view, it makes sense. Why pay a supervisor's salary for those ten minutes, when a lower-paid employee is available. The person who's paid the least should do these types of tasks.

Motivation
Motivating employees to be productive and use all their talents and abilities is one of management's biggest problems. How would you motivate a lethargic employee? Supervisors have to know "what turns the crank" of an employee with low productivity. It's important to learn what motivates each employee so you can utilize their unique talents and abilities as fully as possible.

Time Management
This is important, no matter what position you hold. However, because you're now worth more money per hour, it costs your company more if you waste time. If you can't manage your own time, how can you utilize the time of subordinates effectively? You must be able to manage not only your time but your subordinates' time as well.

Problem Solving and Decision Making
People often "spin their wheels" because they're trying to solve the wrong problem. They spend hours working on a particular problem instead of standing back from it to determine whether that is the *real* problem. They need to learn the techniques necessary to define and solve complicated problems. Many women excel at creative problem solving. Make use of these talents.

Meeting Skills
Most supervisors spend a considerable portion of their time in meetings. Unless meetings are conducted correctly, they just turn out to be time wasters for everyone involved. Learning how to chair a meeting correctly and handle problem attendees is essential for supervisors.

Interpersonal Skills
Many seminars and workshops are offered on this topic because management realizes the importance of good communication skills at all levels of business. Training normally covers such skills as: speaking, listening, writing, reading body language, and understanding why you and others behave as you do.

Employee Discipline
Most new supervisors (and even seasoned ones) hate disciplining their subordinates or, especially, having to fire one. They hate being the "heavy."

Often supervisors bring out the worst rather than the best in their employees simply because they use ineffective tactics to correct the behaviour or performance of their subordinates. There are some hard and fast rules of discipline (including laws that protect employees from wrongful dismissal). Supervisors who don't learn to discipline correctly may find themselves in court defending themselves and/or their company.

Interviewing Techniques
If you have the responsibility of choosing your staff, training in interviewing will help you write advertisements, screen applications, prepare for an interview, and determine what questions to ask in the interview (as well as what questions *not* to ask because they're illegal). This training also emphasizes the importance of proper reference checking and gives guidance on how to choose the best person for the position.

PRIORITY 1 – OBTAIN SUPERVISORY TRAINING
If you're a supervisor and don't have the proper training, I urge you to make that a top priority. If you're not yet a supervisor but hope to become one, don't wait until a supervisory position is available. Get the training first. That will give you an edge when applying for supervisory positions. If your employer won't pay for this training, look upon it as an investment in your future and pay for it yourself. The techniques aren't hard to learn and once you know the right way to do something, you'll feel more confident. And that can make a big difference.

SOCIALIZING WITH YOUR STAFF
How do you feel about socializing with your subordinates out of the work environment? Supervisors are encouraged to keep their

business and private lives completely separate. If you're going to socialize with people you supervise, you should *never* discuss business while socializing. You're no longer a "buddy," you're a supervisor, with a totally different role to fulfil. Moreover, if you socialize with only two out of your five subordinates, the other three may think you're showing favouritism to the "chosen" two.

Should you entertain your staff at home? This is one area in which there seems to be a double standard. Normal procedure under the heading of "games played in business" is for a supervisor to entertain subordinates at Christmas and perhaps an annual barbeque. When a male supervisor does this, everyone accepts it as a matter of course. If you think you might not feel comfortable in this role, you may have to ask yourself, "Am I going to play this game? Is it to my advantage or to my disadvantage?" You might decide to opt out. On the other hand, it might look bad to your manager that you don't play this game. It might be assumed that you don't have a very good rapport with your staff. You should weigh the relevant factors and make a conscious decision about which route is best for your particular situation. If you decide to sidestep this "obligation," you'll have broken a rule of the game, but at least you'll *know* you've done it.

How about socializing with your own peer group? That's different. It's fine to socialize with them because you'll keep the "old-boy network" going. You'll learn a lot through this grapevine.

PROBLEMS SUPERVISORS HAVE
Problem. Your staff resents the fact that you can get credit for their ideas. They feel that if they do all the legwork and provide all the background information, they should get the credit.
Response. According to Rule No. 15 of the games played in business (explained in Chapter 3) the supervisor has the right to do this. However, in my supervisory classes I encourage participants to give credit where credit is due. Otherwise they're *demotivating* their staff rather than *motivating* them. They will get better work out of their subordinates if they encourage them to come forward with ideas by giving credit for useful contributions. Supervisors should try to guard against fears that subordinates are becoming too good. All supervisors should prepare one or two subordinates to take over their positions. Many supervisors don't understand that unless someone is nipping at their heels and is equipped to

take over their position, they won't be promoted higher in their company themselves.

Problem. "I give indirect supervision to a staff of three. They do sloppy work, but I can't discipline them. My boss does it."

Response. This problem would not occur if you had the full responsibility of a supervisor. You should approach your boss and explain to him or her the kinds of problems this lack of control creates, and ask either to be given a full supervisory role or to have the three employees report directly to your boss. He or she will then delegate and check their work as well as disciplining them.

Problem. "I'm a supervisor, but I have been told I don't have the right to promote the person I think should be promoted. I had two people I was considering for a promotion, and I chose the one I felt was best qualified, but my manager overruled my decision."

Response. Use facts to prove why your decision was the best one, and be willing to stand behind your decision. Because you're closer to these employees than your boss, you know things your boss doesn't. Use these facts to explain your point of view.

Also, ask yourself whether it's a "political" promotion. You may have to bite the bullet and give in because your boss has control over what you do. You'll have to listen to his or her wishes. But do have your say first, before giving in.

Problem. "I want to promote one of my staff into a supervisory role, but my company refuses to give her supervisory training. None of the supervisors in the company have had training in the past, but I think it should be given."

Response. I suggest explaining the company situation to the employee, while also emphasizing the importance to her of obtaining supervisory training. You might point out that she owes it to herself to help herself succeed, even if her company won't. Most educational costs are tax deductible. It should also be kept in mind that a small financial investment now could earn her not only a promotion but future income as well.

Problem. "How should I have handled the first day on a job in which I was now responsible for supervising my former peers?"

Response. If you don't manage to dispel any envy your new subordinates feel in the first week, you're likely to fail. I suggest you call your employees into your office. Have your manager introduce you to your staff as their new supervisor. He or she then leaves and you say: "I know many of you wanted the position I'm now in, and I can't blame you if you feel a little annoyed that I got it instead of you. The company decided that I was the best person for the job. What we do from now on depends on us. I need your support to handle this job properly. In return, I'll do everything I can to see that you're made ready for the next promotional opportunity. Can I count on you for your support?"

Then ask each person in turn for a commitment. Once they've made such a commitment they're more likely to follow through.

If you sense reluctance to make the needed commitment, don't ignore it. Say something like "Margie, you seem hesitant. What can I do to make the situation a little easier for you?"

If an employee still balks, you know this is someone to keep your eye on. Don't be surprised if he or she tries to sabotage your efforts. If this happens, you'll have to be on top of the situation and take immediate disciplinary action. Don't be afraid to do it. Nip the problem in the bud; don't let it grow and flourish and contaminate the others in your section.

COMMUNICATING
Some differences between men and women are the result of conditioning. Others appear to be inherited. In the latter category is the fact that the consequences of a stroke for a woman may often be less serious than for a man, especially in the area of speech functions. Men lose their verbal skills after stroke damage to the left side of the brain (speaking skills), and their conceptual skills when the right side is damaged. For women, only a stroke on the right side will produce slight verbal-skills problems. This difference occurs because in women both the left and the right hemispheres of the brain are involved in verbal and spatial skills.

The brain has two halves, each of which controls the opposite side of the body. Nerve fibres allow the passage of information to flow between the two halves. Women have more nerve fibres passing between the two halves than men do because their passageways are wider and larger in places than men's.

The fact that there's considerable communication between the right and left brains in women may explain why women appear to use both sides together, whereas men rely more on each side for different purposes. This could be one of the reasons why men and women have a difficult time communicating with each other. However, once women accept that such difficulties may arise, they can take steps to avoid communication breakdown.

Women need to make a determined effort to learn "men's language." I always assumed that the same word meant the same thing to both men and women, but my research indicates that this is wrong. For example, in a mixed (men and women) social gathering, I heard a woman in the group discussing her career aspirations. She stated that a job she was considering was a real "challenge."

The man she was with asked her why she didn't turn it down.

She again stated, "I don't want to. As I explained, it's a real challenge."

"Well then, turn it down!" he repeated.

They discussed the issue back and forth and ended up in an argument. The rest of us sat by, wondering what the problem was. It suddenly became apparent to me that they were discussing different things. To clarify matters, I asked each of them to explain to me what the word "challenge" meant to them.

The woman explained that the word "challenge" to her meant that something was exciting, that it gave her a chance to prove herself, to stretch, to reach her full potential (a very positive thing).

Her male partner felt "challenge" meant someone was standing in his way, keeping him from obtaining what he wanted. He felt that, if challenged, he would prepare to do "battle" to overcome the obstruction.

This revelation got the group trying to think of words that meant different things to men and women. We were able to come up with a few, and I'm constantly seeking others. Two examples follow.

Macho. To a woman this means a chauvinistic man who thinks he's "God's gift to women." It may carry connotations of small- or narrow-mindedness and vanity. To a man it suggests a strong, decisive leader, worthy of respect — a trend setter and role model.

Gentle. To a woman this suggests someone tender, empathetic, and in tune with others — someone who does not take advantage of others but is dependable, unassuming, trustworthy and kind. To a man it suggests someone mentally weak, soft and wishy-washy, an indecisive "wimp" — someone who can be pushed around by others, is passive and perhaps physically weak as well.

There are many words we use every day that have these different meanings for men and women.

CLARIFICATION AND PARAPHRASING

If you think a statement you've made might be misinterpreted, use clarification and/or paraphrasing to confirm the meaning. Paraphrasing should be used especially when complex issues are being discussed. We use these techniques all the time in simple situations — for example, when taking a telephone message, to ensure we've heard it correctly. But such clarification should be sought when two people are conversing at any time. If used correctly, it can prevent many misunderstandings. Here is an example:

Marge: "Jill should never have become a nurse."

Bill: "Oh, I thought she was a good nurse."

Marge: "Did I say she wasn't a good nurse?"

In this conversation, Bill's paraphrase has revealed that there's a gap between what Marge meant and what he understood her to say. Marge's statement could have been intended to mean any of the following:

– Jill doesn't like being a nurse.
– Jill doesn't do a good job as a nurse.
– Jill doesn't work well with her patients.
– Jill is more of a detail person than a people person.
– Jill would be better suited to an accounting career.

Bill now knows he's chosen the wrong possibility and asks for clarification.

Marge: "I meant that she is better suited to a position in business. She has such good business sense."

This statement, too, could be interpreted in more than one way:

– Jill has management skills.
– Jill is better suited to a position in which she makes more decisions.
– Jill could do better for herself financially if she were in business.
– Jill is not using her talents and abilities.

Bill's next choice turns out to be correct.

Bill: "Oh, I see, you think Jill is better suited to a position where she makes more decisions?"

Marge: "Exactly! Nursing isn't the right job for Jill."

The need for paraphrasing leading to clarification is clear in this conversation. Initially, Marge believed that Bill knew Jill shouldn't be a nurse because she was better suited to a career in business. Bill, on the other hand, believed Marge had implied that Jill wasn't good at her nursing job.

This kind of problem occurs frequently. If you're not sure what a person means, ask for more information or use paraphrasing to ensure you've understood what was intended. You already use this technique now, though you may not have been aware of it. If anyone has ever said to you, "No, that's not what I meant," you've been using paraphrasing. Use it more often to lessen communication problems.

CHAPTER TEN

HOW TO FEEL GOOD ABOUT YOURSELF

Most of us want to feel good about ourselves.

Many people feel they have to succeed in their careers *before* they can feel good about themselves. But did you know that your *present* level of self-esteem seriously affects your chances of success?

Your self-confidence — or lack of it — affects your behaviour. It can make you passive and socially compliant — sacrificing your own needs at the cost of becoming a doormat. It can make you aggressive — satisfying your own needs at the cost of hurting others. Or it can make you nicely **assertive** — with realistic concern for yourself but also for the needs and feelings of those around you. If others "walk all over you" or you alienate others by your behaviour, your chances of success will be harmed in both cases. But in order to change your approach to others, you may need to change your views about yourself.

BEHAVIOUR STYLES
Our behaviour reveals a great deal about our attitudes both toward ourselves and toward others. There are three basic types of behaviour.
Passive Behaviour
Passive people seldom express their own wants and needs and usually give in to the demands and wants of others. They're reluctant to defend their rights and to stand up for themselves. Their behaviour says they don't respect themselves.

Aggressive Behaviour

Aggressive people show little respect for the needs and wants of others. They expect things to be done their way or not at all. They have difficulty putting themselves in the shoes of others — they lack empathy. They take advantage of others; when a colleague shows weakness, that's when they pounce and go for the kill.

There are two sub-categories of passive and aggressive behaviour.

Passive resistance

Passive-resistant types are passive people who are trying to be more assertive. They mutter and sigh a lot and play manipulative games to get their way. They have not learned to ask for what they want in an up-front manner.

Indirect aggression

These people are somewhere between the assertive and the aggressive type. They use such subtle, underhanded methods to get their way as sabotage, sarcasm, the silent treatment and gossip. They use manipulative games instead of acting assertively.

Assertive Behaviour

Assertive people show by their attitude to others that they respect themselves. They are not afraid to express their needs to others and are willing to defend their rights.

On the other hand, they allow others to express their needs and defend their rights as well.

Assertive is what you want to be most of the time.

Nobody can force another to give up his or her rights. The only person who can give up rights is the one who owns those rights. Unless it's part of the normal give-and-take in relationships, we become less of a person if we give up our rights to someone else.

Many women still follow the traditional behaviour of their mothers and grandmothers. They were taught that passive behaviour is the normal and accepted behaviour for women. Those who compete or become too powerful (an unfeminine trait according to traditionalists) are made to believe they're acting aggressively. In reality, they're acting assertively. Women who succeed in business have had to unlearn their traditional passivity in order to be more assertive. A few have overcompensated, have gone to the other extreme, and have become aggressive.

Let us look at the three types of behaviour in more detail.

PASSIVE BEHAVIOUR

Passive people and those who use passive-resistance often feel:
- angry (because others take advantage of them);
- frustrated (because they seldom get their way);
- withdrawn and defeated (because they feel there's no use in participating or trying when nobody listens to them);
- inferior (because they lack in self-esteem and self-confidence);
- anxious and insecure (because they feel they have little control over their lives).

These feelings may make them irritable, but they often lack the courage to acknowledge their feelings of fear and inadequacy and will try to pretend everything's all right. They don't know how to increase their self-confidence, and the negative feedback they invite often reinforces their poor self-image. They seldom attempt new things and don't take risks because they're afraid they'll fail, and they don't know how to handle failure. They may put themselves down and have difficulty accepting even the simplest compliment. They tend to underestimate the value of what they do. They may seem to lack energy and zest because they are usually doing things that others want them to do, rather than things they have chosen for themselves.

These people believe that while you may be "okay" they are "not okay."

AGGRESSIVE BEHAVIOUR

Aggressive and indirectly aggressive people often feel:
- powerful (in the short run, because they enjoy seeing people scurry and rush to carry out their orders);
- guilty (in the long run, because they know they alienate people and sense that they're taking advantage of others);
- threatened (by those they perceive as "better" than they are).

These feelings may impel them constantly to brag about how good, how intelligent, how strong, etc., they are and to try to make themselves feel important by putting others down. They are "always right" and seem to believe the only ideas worth listening to are their own. They frequently blame others for things that go wrong and are experts at passing the buck. They are often isolated (having alienated everyone around them). They may have a high energy level, but usually their energies are geared in the wrong direction, toward destructive rather than constructive activities.

These people believe they are "okay," but that you are "not okay."

ASSERTIVE BEHAVIOUR
Assertive people often feel:
– optimistic (because they approach new tasks and ideas with a positive rather than a negative attitude);
– calm (because they are at peace with themselves and others);
– enthusiastic (because they expect to succeed);
– satisfied (because they know where they're going and how they're going to get there, and usually attain their goals);
– in control (because they seldom have mood swings that affect their communication with and behaviour toward others);
– self-confident (because they feel they can reach their goals without stealing ideas from others or climbing over others).

These people are able to be honest and direct. They are confident enough to take risks when necessary, but they know their limitations. They're not overwhelmed when they don't succeed at something. They are not afraid to acknowledge their own failings or feelings about what others' behaviour is doing to them. They are able to respect other people and to accept respect in return. They frequently have a lot of energy, which they are able to channel in the right direction.

These people feel that they are "okay," and that you are "okay" too.

CONSEQUENCES OF THE MAIN BEHAVIOURAL STYLES
It's important to know what each kind of behaviour does to those around you and how they're likely to react to your particular behavioural style.

Passive behaviour often brings out other people's aggressive tendencies, and they don't like the resulting guilt feelings. For example, suppose you have to work overtime unexpectedly. Jane (another mother, with a child in day-care), picks up your daughter and looks after her until you come home. Lately you've had considerable overtime. Jane has never asked for the same favour in return. You've offered to baby-sit in the evenings or weekends, but

Jane hasn't taken you up on this. She's a very passive person who lets people take advantage of her, and you feel guilty because you feel you're acting aggressively. So, to alleviate these guilt feelings, you make alternative child-care arrangements and don't have much contact with Jane any more.

Jane alienated your friendship by allowing you to take advantage of her (which was exactly the opposite of what she intended). Passive people such as Jane must realize what they do to others and stop acting passively! She may have believed she was pleasing you by never asking a favour in return. The last thing she wanted to do was alienate you, but that's exactly what she did.

Passive behaviour, therefore, may make other people feel:
- angry (because they wish you could ask for what you need and make decisions for yourself);
- frustrated and impatient (because it bothers them when you refuse all their attempts to help or to even things up);
- threatened (because your negative attitude makes it difficult for them to maintain their own positive thinking);
- disrespectful (because you don't respect yourself enough to stand up for what you believe in).

Aggressive behaviour may make the people around you feel:
- threatened and angry (because you try to make yourself look good by attacking them and putting them down);
- frustrated (because they have to expend so much energy just defending themselves from your abuse);
- resentful (because you have acquired power over them by unfair means);
- defensive (because they expect you to attack);
- hurt (by your sarcasm, silent treatment and putdowns);
- humiliated (because you correct them and/or try to make them look foolish in front of others).

Assertive behaviour may make the people around you feel:
- positive (because your positive, confident attitude is infectious);
- safe (because they trust you);
- satisfied (because you are capable of noticing *their* good points as well as your own);
- co-operative (because you know how to make them feel good about themselves, so they enjoy working with you);
- respected (because you're willing to listen to their views and don't have to have things go your own way all the time);

– energetic (because there are no games being played, and they're able to use their energy constructively).

Do passive people usually achieve their goals?
No, because they seldom have goals in the first place.

Do aggressive people usually achieve their goals?
Sometimes in the short run, but they invite retaliation in the long run.

Do assertive people usually achieve their goals?
Yes. Their aim is not to win at others' expense but to achieve their goals by finding solutions that benefit everyone.

MANIPULATION

Men and women often get their way by manipulating others. Manipulation is closely related to games playing. If you are an obvious manipulator or games player you may have trouble getting people to trust you. Or, perhaps you use manipulative tactics or play games without realizing it. If you think this could be the case, a book such as *Games People Play*, by Eric Berne, may help you identify your games — and stop playing them.

As an alternative to assertiveness, such manipulative plays as passive-resistance (complaining, whining, dragging your feet but never directly stating your grievance to your boss) are ineffective and create bad feelings. If you want a raise, be assertive. Ask for an appointment to talk to your boss, and explain that (for example) you've worked for the company for fifteen months without a performance appraisal or a salary review (or whatever the case may be) and that you think you deserve a raise.

CONFIDENCE IN SPEAKING

Verbal fluency is essential for you to progress in business. In order to say what you want, you have to feel assertive enough to express your point. If you aren't sure what you want to say, it will show in your speaking style. Most supervisors and managers have to make group presentations. If you freeze up, you're in trouble.

Your body language is also important. Men's voices tend to deepen when they're nervous; women's become shrill or breathless. Many women hunch over when they're nervous. This reduces their lung capacity and makes it harder to project their voices. A man is more likely to assume a defiant posture — shoulders straight, chest out, head up — when nervous. This expands the chest and gives the voice more volume. Try this if you have to project your voice.

When making public presentations women often appear tense as though trying to take up as little space as possible. Their shoulders and arms may appear stiff. Their hands may flutter to their faces when they're not sure of a point. Raised eyebrows and a forward-leaning posture suggest that they're looking for approval. The whole body is asking, "Do you like what I'm saying?"

Many women rely heavily on qualifying phrases, such as "I guess," "I believe," or "I think," and end sentences with a question — for example, "Wouldn't that be a good idea?" Again, they appear to be seeking approval. This sort of presentation suggests uncertainty and indecisiveness.

If this describes you, try using a tape recorder to check your voice pattern, or better yet, use a video camera to identify things that need improvement. Ask friends to assess your speeches. Practise, practise and practise some more, until you *know* you're going to do a good job. Self-confidence is half the battle when giving a presentation. (The other half is to be properly prepared, with facts to back up your views.)

SELF-SABOTAGE

Sometimes we fail to get ahead because, without realizing it, we are sabotaging ourselves. There's a "little twerp" inside us who asks maliciously, "Who do you think you are?" and questions our every action. When these doubts take over, they cause us to focus on some little thing we've done wrong and block the good feelings we have after a job well done.

Or we dwell on our disadvantages, saying such things as: "If only I were younger, older, thinner, more beautiful, smarter, a better dresser, could talk better, sing better, dance better". Or: "I should have stayed at school and got my degree"; "I should have made a job change years ago"; "I should have taken that promotion when it was offered to me!" Don't "should" on yourself! If you focus on the negatives in life instead of remembering the good things you have done and may still do, you're letting yourself down. Be a good friend to yourself.

At the same time, it may not be enough consciously to aim for a positive attitude if fears you're not aware of are bothering you. If you can identify the fears that are holding you back, you can find ways of dealing with them that will allow you to progress.

Fear of Success

The reasons for self-sabotaging behaviour can be quite complex. Perhaps you suspect that if you take risks and become a success you might somehow lose the love of people who are important to you. Men regard their work as a duty; they do not assume that their wives will withhold love if taxed by the demands of *their* husband's work. They don't assume, either, that their wives will be jealous of their success. But most women are not convinced that they're owed unwavering love by a husband who may be inconvenienced or challenged by their work.

Such women may be afraid to succeed. This is often a subconscious fear, and the things they do to sabotage themselves are well camouflaged. Analyse your thoughts and behaviour to see if this is happening to you.

1. Do you think you'll be seen as less feminine if you succeed? Successful females often appear to be far more competitive than the average women, and you may feel uncomfortable in this role. You think men who feel intimidated by successful women may give putdowns that you can't handle.
2. Do you think you'll have to choose between being successful in a career and finding a spouse or mate? Or that if you're successful you may lose the mate you already have? You may feel you can have one or the other, but not both. But many have both.
3. Do you worry that if you choose to start climbing, you'll feel obliged to keep climbing until you overreach yourself and fail? You'd hate to fail. Some feel this would be worse than not trying in the first place.

Fear of Failure

Women often turn down excellent opportunities and are unsure why they've done so. If you have this happen to you, ask yourself, "Why am I not taking this opportunity? Is fear of failure holding me back? Or is it lack of money, connections, time or child care?"

Learn to analyse why you're being your own worst enemy.

Fear of failure can help you convince yourself that you are incapable of handling more responsibility. It encourages you to think of every situation in which you can't possibly measure up, and to turn down the promotion because of those fears. If you do accept the position without dealing with these negative feelings, you're probably setting yourself up to fail.

If this is your problem, keep in mind that you're capable of far more than you think. I recommend that you never take a promotion to a position in which you know every aspect of the job. If you do this, you're already overqualified for the position. All promotional opportunities should leave you room to grow and learn while on the job or through additional training.

Guilt

Guilt is hard to turn off. For example, Georgia went on short business trips to other cities. On one occasion she realized she was feeling uneasy. She thought, "Why am I here, alone — and not with my family? I miss, need and want my husband and kids." She was ashamed of those feelings, so she altered them by turning them around to, "My husband and kids miss, need and want me, and right now I'm letting them down." She felt guilty that her family could not always come first with her. She'd been conditioned to believe that this had to be her role. To change her outlook, she assessed her guilt feelings, realized what had caused them, dealt with them, then turned them off as not being realistic.

LEARNING TO TAKE RISKS

Webster's New World Dictionary defines the word "risk" as "the chance of injury, damage or loss."

It takes courage to take risks, but life without risk is very mundane and boring. Nothing ventured, nothing gained. Some fear not being able to "pull it off" — that they'll fail. They've been taught that failure's a bad thing, so in taking risks they're facing the possibility of ending up with not one but two bad things: failure at what they've attempted to do, and the added burden of lowered self-esteem.

Often racehorses win only by a "nose." Why do we assume that we can't just win by a nose at what we attempt. We really don't have to be that much better than everyone else — just a "nose" better. To think otherwise means we're expecting ourselves to be superhuman.

Think of things you don't do well. How do you know you don't do these things well?

For instance, perhaps you think you're not good at sports. But when was the last time you tested your abilities in this area? Perhaps you're letting a failure you had as a child or teenager limit your adult life needlessly?

Let's say that as a child you spilled your milk, tripped often, bumped into furniture and dropped things. You were never able to forget these "failings" because you were reminded of them over and over by your parents, siblings and friends, until you began to believe you were as "awkward" as they said you were. This then became a self-fulfilling prophecy. Thereafter, whenever you attempted something that took dexterity or co-ordination, you didn't bother trying because the old tapes that said you were clumsy kept playing in your brain. You simply decided that you still couldn't do it and didn't even give it a try.

Analyse yourself. Do you have any negative tapes buzzing around in your brain that may be stopping you from trying something new? Test your abilities. Perhaps you're more capable than the negative tapes in your subconscious say you are.

I always approach new things with an open mind. When approaching a new task, I think, "I've never tried this before, but I'll try my best." If I don't do well at it, and I know I've given it my best try, I've learned that this is something I really don't do well, and I can go on to something else. If I *do* succeed at the task, the positive results usually spur me on to try other new things. With this positive approach, I find that I succeed at about three out of every five things I attempt — and the ratio is improving.

Do you let yourself feel that you have "failed" at something when you have given it a good effort? Why not try telling yourself that it was a learning experience. Take the word "failure" out of your vocabulary. You can't be good at everything! If you think you have to be, you're bound to spend most of your life in misery.

If you're holding off taking action because you're afraid to take the risk, do the following:
1. Define as closely as possible what you think the risk is.
2. Determine what you could gain emotionally and physically by making the attempt.

3. Determine what you could lose emotionally and physically by making the attempt.
4. Try to ascertain if you need more information before deciding to take the risk. Where would you obtain this information? Who has this kind of information?
5. What's the best thing that could happen if you took the chance and attempted it?
6. What's the worst thing that could happen if you took the chance and attempted it?
7. How could you lessen the risk?
8. Is it now worth taking the risk?

Do you over- or underemphasize the consequences of everything you do? Have you hurt others in the past by acting too soon, with too little information? By analysing what your action will do to others or how it will affect other projects, you'll be less likely to goof again.

ACCEPTING COMPLIMENTS

Do you have trouble fielding compliments? When someone makes favourable comments about your outfit, do you find yourself replying, "Oh, this old rag?" We often discount or refuse to accept another's kind words. If you deserve the compliment, learn how to accept it with grace. If you can't accept it, what are you telling the person who pays you the compliment? That's right — you're calling them a liar or a poor judge of character. You're giving them a putdown. After all, they meant their comment to make *you* feel better, not to make *them* feel bad. You're likely to receive few compliments from that person in the future, and we all need authentic praise to survive. The only compliments you should discount are "marshmallows." These are sickly sweet, manipulative remarks that simply aren't true, or grossly exaggerate the truth.

HOW TO INCREASE SELF-ESTEEM

If your self-image is drooping, I sincerely urge you to attend a good assertiveness-training class. It can change your life. Ask around, check course outlines, and attend one that you think will meet your particular needs.

The most important assertive quality you can possess is that of being a positive thinker.

Positive Thinkers believe they will succeed because . . .

Negative Thinkers believe they will fail because . . .

Positive thinkers have taken the time to look at themselves objectively. They know what they do well. They find as many opportunities to exercise their talents as possible because to do so gives them good feelings about themselves. They're also aware of things they don't do well. But instead of sweeping this knowledge under the rug, they do something to improve their ability.

You can help yourself be a positive thinker by doing the following:

1. Make a list of people you associate with on a regular basis. Make three headings:
   (A) Positive thinkers
   (B) Negative thinkers
   (C) Those who are right in the middle (Don't have too many people in this category.)
2. Determine the percentage of time you spend with each person. For instance, if you spend seven hours a day with four different people at work, you will probably spend about twenty percent with each of them during the week. (You'll end up with a total well over 100 percent, but don't worry about that.)
3. Determine whether you're spending more time with positive- or negative-thinking people.
4. Now rate yourself. Are you basically a positive or negative thinker?

To help you with number 4, ask yourself these questions (the more yes answers you have the better):

A. Do you think of yourself as happy?
B. Are you surprised when a friend lets you down?
C. Do you believe the human race will survive past the twentieth century?
D. When you think back over the past few months, do you tend to remember your little successes before your failures and setbacks?
E. If you made a list of your ten favourite people, would you be on it?
F. Do you feel comfortable making yourself the butt of your own jokes?
G. When the unexpected forces you to change your plans, are you quick to spot the hidden advantages in the new situation?

H. When you catch a stranger staring at you, do you decide it's because he or she finds you attractive?
I. Do you like most of the people you meet?
J. When you think about next year, do you tend to think you'll be better off than you are now?
K. Do you often stop to admire things of beauty or interest?
L. When someone finds fault with you for something you've done, can you tell the difference between useful (positive) criticism and the kind of griping that is better ignored?
M. Do you praise your best friend more often than you criticize him or her?

Do you spend too much time with negative thinkers? If so, you may have to reduce the time you spend with them so you can either become a positive thinker or help yourself to stay one. If you work in an environment where you have to deal with negative-thinking clients, it's essential for you to spend your time *away from work* with positive-thinking friends and family.

One participant in my "Create a Positive Image" seminar wrote to me afterwards to describe what she did to change the people she worked with (including herself) from negative to positive thinkers. When she arrived back at work after attending my seminar, she asked her co-workers to help her become a more positive person. She asked them to catch her whenever she was using negative thinking. Oddly enough this worked for the whole group. They all began catching each other when they were using negative thinking. About a month later, their boss called a staff meeting at which he said, "I don't know what you're doing differently, but keep it up!" You can help co-workers, friends and family by using this technique. Or you could ask them if they would like you to help them be more positive thinkers.

If you're presently unemployed, it can be difficult to think positively, even if this is your normal frame of mind. I've advised people who attend my "Get that Job!" seminar that their attitude, (positive or negative), has a direct bearing on whether they're hired or not. Employers are looking for positive thinkers, and given the choice, wouldn't you be too?

Positive thinking requires imagination, the ability to visualize yourself succeeding, and the belief that you can do it!

If you expect to fail — you will. If you believe you can succeed and work to achieve your goal, your chances of success are good.

SUPPORT GROUPS

Having a support group is essential for positive living. Whom would you call on if you'd had a bad day and needed someone to help you through it? Everyone needs someone to support them when they're down. If you don't have at least two of these people in your life, figure out how you can get them. They're essential for good mental health.

SELF-IMAGE

There are many other things you can do to improve your self-esteem and self-image. Here are some of them:
1. Write a list of things you like about yourself.
2. Write a list of things you do well. (Bring these lists out when your self-esteem is lagging.)
3. Write a list of things you dislike about yourself. Ask yourself how you could change these dislikes to likes?
4. Write a list of things you would like to do better.

The next step is to set some goals to improve your lot in life using the list as a guide. Ask yourself what you are doing to build on your good points. Are you regularly using your unique talents?

I've always been an excellent swimmer, and I swim whenever I get the chance. For years I had a vague fantasy of becoming a scuba diver. As the years passed, the fantasy became more and more fuzzy. One day, after I had written down things I had wanted to accomplish in my lifetime, I found that this was one goal I really wanted to achieve. So (rather late in life), I took up scuba diving and have spent many happy hours in the briny deep. What have *you* been putting off? Don't you think it's about time you did it?

HOW TO DRESS IN BUSINESS

This topic has been discussed to death, but I'd like to add my two-cents' worth. I always advise women to dress the way women at a level above them do. For instance — if you're a secretary, dress as if you're an executive secretary. If you're in line for a supervisory position, dress like a supervisor, even before you obtain the position. It's amazing what a difference this makes to your chances for promotion. If you look the part, you're not as likely to be over-looked. You'll feel much better about yourself as well.

We get so many conflicting pieces of advice on how a woman

should dress in business that it can cause a lot of confusion. My suggestion is to dress with femininity and *class.* I don't mean high fashion (that costs too much money and is often not suitable for office wear). Choose feminine (and I do stress feminine) suits, or wear simple dresses that flatter your figure type. Stay clear of wild geometric stripes and flowers. Ruffles are okay as long as they're not of the "little girl" or "dance-hall madam" variety. Use jewellery sparingly, and avoid dangling earrings.

Choose an easy-to-care-for hairstyle, and if your hair is long, pin it up; otherwise men will see you as a woman first and an executive second.

HOW DO YOU LET PEOPLE KNOW YOU'RE A POSITIVE THINKER?

- Let your clothing, appearance, posture and even the gleam in your eyes tell people you like and respect yourself.
- Try to associate with other positive thinkers.
- Pursue things you're good at, work at things you'd like to be good at, and explore things you might turn out to be good at.
- Learn from your mistakes.
- Keep an open mind about your own and other people's ideas, and don't dwell on what "might have been."
- Learn to sense when your chances of success are good in order to persevere with a project. (In the sporting terminology of the business world, learn to know when you're "on a roll." Or learn how to tell when it's time to "take the ball and run with it.")

CHAPTER ELEVEN

HOW TO WORK EFFECTIVELY WITH MALE SUPERIORS, PEERS AND SUBORDINATES

WHY ARE SOME MEN INTIMIDATED BY ASSERTIVE WOMEN?

How might a man feel when confronted by a woman in what he thinks of as *male* territory at work?

Let's say you're a man working in your backyard (workplace), and you spot a strange animal (a female manager) in your yard. This animal isn't like those you normally find in these surroundings. You know you've seen this type of animal in another environment (support position) but don't quite know how it will behave in the present situation. You're rightfully careful. You don't make any moves toward it (ignore the new female manager) but merely stand back and study it. If it shows anger or defensiveness toward you, you get ready to defend yourself.

This is the effect a woman has on a man when she enters a male-dominated work environment. The man doesn't know whether the woman is dangerous or not. She seems to be doing things that don't make sense, and he has a hard time figuring her out. Naturally he's on the defensive! Women in management must try to understand men's inner turmoil and help them adapt by earning their trust and respect. They should not expect immediate acceptance.

To continue with our hypothetical situation, you (the man) are still standing back, studying the animal. You have your defenses

144

up, so that you're ready to protect yourself if necessary. When the animal (the woman) makes funny sideways moves toward you (feminine behaviour) you're even more wary.

Now the animal helps itself to some tidbit (part of your job) off your patio table. You're naturally annoyed. (This is what some women do — they do part of someone else's job thinking they're helping.)

I could go on with this comparison, but I think you get the drift.

A variety of things may cause men to be intimidated by an assertive woman.

Heaven forbid, she may be better than he is! It's almost impossible for a man to visualize himself reporting to a woman. He thinks of the woman supervisor or manager as a mother figure — but he's a big boy now! He also might be intimidated by the fact that he doesn't know where she's coming from — she plays by a different set of rules.

Colleen was given a senior position, with several men reporting to her. One man objected because he had applied for her position. His behaviour bordered on insubordination, and Colleen had to deal with it. She said to him privately, "I know you wanted my position, John, and I can relate to how you must feel. I too know what it feels like to be overlooked for a promotion. I want and need your co-operation, but I won't tolerate any more negative behaviour from you. Can I count on you to change this?"

His behaviour improved, and he became a good employee. Later, Colleen helped John identify why he had not been given her supervisory position. She was able to make sure he obtained the necessary training to equip him for the next promotional opportunity.

Men who feel intimidated by women often refer to them in derogatory ways, putting them in their "place." They say, "She's pushy," or, "She's castrating." If there's a man in your life who seems to be intimidated, it's important for you to try to understand the situation. He may feel attacked and decide to defend himself. If you are unaware that you've intimidated him, you will be shocked when he uses defensive tactics. If this happens, ask yourself what you've done to "rock the boat" for him. Reassure him that you don't want to invade his turf, but that you just want space of your own.

WORKING FOR AN AGGRESSIVE BOSS

Aggressive bosses haven't learned one of the basic fundamentals of supervision. You can't push subordinates into doing a good job for you, you have to lead them. A boss who disciplines employees publicly (or labels them rather than dealing with their behaviour) is bound to fail.

But what can you, as an employee, do? Tell him — that's what! Learn how to use feedback (explained in Chapter 7) to let him know what his behaviour is doing to you. This takes nerve, but most bosses will look up to you for having the courage to do it. For example, if your boss has disciplined you publicly, wait until he has calmed down and ask for five minutes of his time. Say something like, "I have a problem, and I need your help in solving it. When you discipline me in front of my co-workers, I feel humiliated. Did you intend me to feel that way?" Then add, "I hope you understand that if you do this in the future, I'll walk away from you."

If your boss labels you, rather than your behaviour, again I suggest you talk to him privately. Say, "I have a problem, and I need your help in solving it. I find it difficult to handle the putdowns you've been giving me lately. If you have a beef, discipline me, but don't call me names. I can't defend my actions when you call me names. Telling me that I made a mistake in setting up the marketing plan for the Carter account allows me to change my behaviour. The way it is now, I don't know how to improve my performance or what you really want of me. Can I count on you to do this for me?"

Under no circumstances go to *his* boss and complain. If the situation doesn't change, put up with it while working for a transfer to another position in the company or leave for greener pastures. When you feel your boss is removing all the pride and pleasure you get from your work, it's time to leave.

One seminar participant asked how she could handle a situation in which, as a supervisor, she was regarded as aggressive when she felt she was just standing up for her rights. She was a very forceful, self-assured individual. I suggested that it could be her tone of voice or her body language. By moderating commands ("Do this.") into requests ("I'd like you to . . ."), she could leave her staff with a much gentler impression.

Another participant's supervisor wanted to know all about her personal life when she didn't want to talk about it. She felt this caused hard feelings. I advised her to keep refusing, but as tactfully as possible: e.g., "I prefer to keep a strong division between my private and business life. I've found it's better for me." Further pressure from her boss could be regarded as aggressive behaviour that should be challenged: "Why is my private life so important to you?" The person should be asked to account for the aggression.

HOW TO DEAL WITH MALE CHAUVINISM
There are two forms of male chauvinism. The first kind is blatant. You *know* this man is out to make you feel bad — to keep you in your "place." The other is more subtle and is done by men who often aren't even aware their actions could be classified as chauvinistic. These are usually older men, or men whose upbringing or home situation has conditioned them to think of women as always in subservient positions. Many of these men call women "dear" because women *are* dear to them. They feel protective toward women and believe it's the man's duty to be the decision maker.

I once worked with a man of this type. He called me into his office one morning and pointed to an article in our local tabloid that told men not to call their female employees "dear" or "honey." He did this all the time, although he would never have intentionally hurt anyone's feelings, and he was afraid that he might have offended his female staff. I had to assure him that in his case he had caused no hard feelings. Because this type of chauvinism isn't meant to hurt women, a gentle response to it is advisable. These men normally don't know that what they do or say may be offensive to you. Unless you let them know there's a problem, they're not going to change. Use feedback to give them the opportunity to change their behaviour.

How should you respond to intentional chauvinism? Men who are blatantly chauvinistic are often sarcastic. When people use hurting sarcasm, it's because they want to put others down.

Why do you think they do this? Because it makes *them* feel more important. The game continues when you respond defensively. Responding with equal sarcasm or getting angry just plays into their hands — so don't do it!

I suggest you analyse why this person feels so inferior that he has to put you down to feel good about himself. Once you have an idea of why this is so, you'll be able to pity him rather than get upset or angry. Don't react to chauvinism. Turn it off; tune it out. Think to yourself, "It's too bad this man feels so inadequate he has to put me down to make himself feel good." Remain calm. The true chauvinist can't handle this — he doesn't know what to do, because you're not playing the game and it's no fun any more. Next time, smile when he's putting you down, and he won't understand what's going on. One woman solved this problem by picturing the offending person wearing a diaper and sitting in a high chair banging a spoon.

If you can't stay quiet or you feel a remark demands a response, try asking something like: "Your last comment was very sarcastic and a putdown. Putdowns hurt. Can you explain why you said what you did?" Or, "Why do you feel you have to give me a putdown like that?" Make the aggressive person account for his actions.

SEXUAL HARASSMENT
Research indicates that seventy to eighty percent of women have experienced one or more forms of sexual harassment while working. Fifty-two percent have lost a job because of it. This is one work problem that's bothered women for centuries. However, the situation is changing slowly as laws across the country are updated.

Definition
Sexual harassment can include one or more of the following:
- unwelcome sexual remarks — e.g., jokes, innuendoes, teasing, verbal abuse;
- taunts about a person's body, attire, age, marital status;
- displays of pornographic, offensive or derogatory pictures;
- practical jokes that cause awkwardness or embarrassment;
- unwelcome invitations or requests, whether indirect or explicit;
- intimidation;
- leering or suggestive gestures;
- condescension or paternalism that undermines self-respect; and
- unnecessary physical contact — e.g., touching, patting, pinching, punching or physical assault.

A complaint of sexual harassment does not necessarily mean sexual harassment has actually taken place. An organization can be held liable for a case of reverse discrimination; that's when an employee fails to receive merited promotions and bonuses that are granted instead to a co-worker in return for sexual favours given to a supervisor.

Here's an example of sexual harassment. Millie had a problem with her male boss who hauled his female employees into his office once or twice a week and bawled them out using profane language. Alberta's sexual harassment policy states that if others object, men and women in the workplace are not to use words (four-letter or otherwise) that have sexual connotations. This policy applies equally to men and women. If *you* use foul language on the job and other employees object to your actions, *you* can be charged with sexual harassment whether you're male or female.

THE LEGAL YO-YO

Two recent court rulings directly affect women who have been sexually harassed or discriminated against.

In November 1986, a landmark ruling handed down from the highest court in Manitoba eliminated human-rights protection against sexual harassment in the workplace. The court also said, "Employers are *not* responsible for acts of discrimination in their workplace unless it can be proven they had a specific policy to discriminate. To be liable, an employer must personally be an accomplice to the act of discrimination or it must be proven that there was a corporate policy to discriminate. It's quite impossible to impose a legal duty on an employer to provide a workplace free of sexual harassment."

This was a big step backward for women. The Manitoba Court of Appeal demonstrated its clear hostility to the purpose and rule of human-rights legislation and rendered the legislation unworkable. According to this court, the sexual harassment women encounter in the workplace is *not* covered by human-rights legislation unless the act specifically says so. Most courts have been trying sexual harassment cases under the sexual discrimination section of the act. This would no longer be allowed.

In B.C., Alberta, Saskatchewan, New Brunswick, Nova Scotia and P.E.I., as well as Manitoba, women have *no* protection against sexual harassment (unless they can get the police to come into the workplace and lay assault charges)! Also, since *employers are not responsible for any acts of discrimination in the workplace,* even if you can prove you were denied a job because of race, disability, age or sex — the employer would not be responsible, nor would the person who committed the act, unless you had hard evidence (tape-recorded, written, etc.) that the act of discrimination was the employer's policy.

Following this decision, the Manitoba attorney-general, Roland Penner, said that his government would amend the Human Rights Act to prohibit sexual harassment specifically.

In July 1987, the Supreme Court of Canada stepped in and ruled that sexual harassment *is* a form of sex discrimination and that employers *are* responsible for the actions of their employees. It also confirmed the amendment to the Canadian Human Rights Act (1983) that makes employers responsible when their workers discriminate on the basis of sex, race, colour, religion or other grounds.

Most human rights commissions have guidelines as to what constitutes sexual harassment, but this doesn't necessarily mean that such guidelines will hold up in a court of law. These should be written laws, not policies. Women need to push for these kinds of laws in their provinces. In the meantime, they should also learn what constitutes sexual harassment in their area, whom to complain to, and how they can eliminate and/or deal with sexual harassment in the future. Companies should be encouraged to post their sexual harassment policy so that all employees will understand where their company stands on the issue. If the company doesn't have such a policy — ask for one.

Various cases from across Canada suggest that, with the proper documentation, a sexual harassment action can succeed:

A waitress who quit her job because of sexual harassment received a $700 settlement from her former employer.

The waitress was subjected to continuous and unsolicited advances from a director of the restaurant she worked at. The director made sexual requests and suggestions and touched her. She objected to his actions, but he persisted.

As a result of the harassment, she quit her job and lodged a complaint with the commission. The restaurant agreed to settle with the complainant after the commission had investigated the complaint, which was corroborated by five employees who witnessed the harassment or had experienced similar treatment.

Three managers of a large Alberta company received a total of $29,600 after the company's owner threatened them for supporting a complainant's allegations of sexual harassment against the general manager.

A female employee of the company complained to her human rights commission that she had been sexually harassed by the general manager. After the three company managers had supported her claim during an investigation by the commission, the owner intimidated them and threatened to sue them for defaming the general manager's character.

The three managers decided to leave the company. They complained to the commission, which mediated settlements of $10,000, $9,000 and $10,600 from the company because the general manager had discriminated against them for assisting in the prosecution of a complaint.

A female bar attendant and a lounge waitress working in an Alberta hotel won compensation from the hotel's management for lost wages suffered because of sexual harassment.

The employees complained to the hotel's assistant manager about unwanted sexual advances from their male supervisor. After the women complained, the hotel reduced the hours of one of the employees. The other was temporarily laid off while the lounge was being renovated but was not contacted or rehired when renovations were completed.

The women received cash settlements of $1,400 each.

A Truro, Nova Scotia, doctor was found guilty of sexual discrimination against a former female employee.

The doctor was found guilty of touching the legs, breasts and buttocks of a female employee during her employment from July to December 1982 at a computer store owned by the doctor. The former employee was awarded almost $1,400.

HOW TO HANDLE SEXUAL HARASSMENT
If you are the object of sexual harassment, take the following steps:
1.   Tell the harasser that you object to whatever he or she is doing or saying. Really mean it! If the person doesn't appear to be

listening, point out that the comment or act is classified as sexual harassment, and you expect it to stop immediately. Make sure you document what happened in case it happens again.

2. If the same thing (or something similar) happens again, repeat your earlier objections and back it up with a written letter or memo. Refer to your earlier verbal complaints. Make several copies of this letter.
    – Send one copy to the offending person
    – Send one to his or her boss, your boss, and the chief executive officer of your company, if you think it's appropriate
    – Keep one copy for your records

3. If the behaviour continues, lodge a formal complaint with your local human rights commission.

NOTE: If the first incident is serious enough, take all three steps at once — object verbally, send a letter (with copies to relevant parties) and lodge a formal complaint with the human rights commission.

DISCRIMINATION AGAINST WOMEN

Here are several examples of actual cases that have been tried (they do not seem to have been affected by the Manitoba legislation mentioned earlier):

A woman who was fired because she was pregnant was compensated by her former employer on grounds of sex discrimination.

The female employee of a rural municipality, hired for a three-month summer position, was fired before her job term expired. Her supervisor said he did not wish to be responsible if she were to have a miscarriage as a result of doing the work, which included mowing lawns, removing weeds, painting and picking up garbage. However, her doctor was aware of her employment and felt it posed no danger to her pregnancy.

The human rights commission, which mediated the settlement, found in its investigation that the complaint was merited. The case was settled when the municipality agreed to pay the employee $935 in compensation.

An Alberta company paid a former employee $2,775 for having discriminated against her on the grounds of sex and marital status.

The employee had worked at the same company as her husband for more than six years, even though the company's policy prohibited hiring more than one person from a family. The company was aware when it hired her that she was married to one of its employees. When the company eventually decided to enforce its policy by firing the woman, she filed her complaint and won.

WHERE TO GO FOR HELP WITH DISCRIMINATION OR HARASSMENT COMPLAINTS

Contact these provincial headquarters for information about the location of your nearest human rights commission office:

Newfoundland
Newfoundland Human
Rights Commission
c/o Department of Justice
P.O. Box 4750
St. John's, Nfld.
A1C 5T7

Nova Scotia
Nova Scotia Human
Rights Commission
P.O. Box 2221
Lord Nelson Arcade
Halifax, N.S.
B3J 3C4

New Brunswick
New Brunswick Human
Rights Commission
P.O. Box 6000
Fredericton, N.B.
E3B 5H1

Prince Edward Island
Prince Edward Island
Human Rights Commission
P.O. Box 2000
180 Richmond St.
Charlottetown, P.E.I.
C1A 7N8

Quebec
Quebec Human
Rights Commission
Mezzanine, 360 rue Saint-Jacques
Montreal, Que.
H2Y 1P5

Ontario
Ontario Human
Rights Commission
400 University Ave.
Toronto, Ont.
M7A 1T7

Manitoba
Manitoba Human
Rights Commission
1007-330 Portage Ave.
Winnipeg, Man.
R3C 0C4

Saskatchewan
Saskatchewan Human
Rights Commission
Ste. 802-224-4 Ave. S.
Saskatoon, Sask.
S7H 2H6

Alberta
Alberta Human
Rights Commission
801-10011-109 St.
Edmonton, Alta.
T5J 3S8

Northwest Territories
Department of Justice and
Public Services
Government of N.W.T.
P.O. Box 1320
Yellowknife, N.W.T.
X1A 2L9

Canada
Canadian Human Rights
Commission
90 Sparks St.
Ottawa, Ont.
K1A 1E1

British Columbia
Human Rights Council
of British Columbia
4000 Seymour Pl.
Victoria, B.C.
V8S 4X8

Yukon
Department of Justice
P.O. Box 2703
Whitehorse, Y.T.
X1A 2C6

CHAPTER TWELVE

OFFICE AND TRAVEL TIPS FOR NEW MANAGERS

RULES FOR FEMALE ROOKIES

Let's say you've been given that golden opportunity and are now in your first supervisory or management position. Here are some tips that will keep you from falling on your face:

- Climb the ladder one step at a time. Otherwise you'll miss important training and information.
- If you receive a promotion, you should also receive a change in office size and location. Ask to see your new office before accepting the new position. Women are usually content with second-rate offices of lowly status. Read up on how status works in an office. The rugs and furniture, the size of the office, whether it has a window, and whether it's a corner office are all important (at least to men) and will identify to others your status in the company.
- When you obtain a promotion, don't keep looking up to your supervisor for direction — learn to make decisions for each situation based on the facts. Learn to research every decision you make.
- Find out if someone you now supervise applied for your new job. Take this person out to lunch soon and ask for his or her co-operation. Explain you'll do everything in your power to make sure he or she is ready for the next promotion that comes along.
- Learn whom to trust and whom not to trust. Don't make friends before getting the "lie of the land." Try talking to the person

who's just left your new position. Find out what hidden problems exist that you may have to solve.

- Try not to make even minor changes until you've been on the job for at least two weeks.
- Don't have recognizably "female" equipment in your office. This includes typewriters, files and records. Refrain from doing duties that would be classified as "secretarial," even though it may save you time. If you feel you still need to use a typewriter occasionally, try to get an extra one in your department that anyone can use when a rush job has to be done. It's also handy to have that extra typewriter available should another go on the fritz. If you continue doing these clerical tasks, your company will likely object.
- Don't use an apologetic attitude when you give work to secretaries. They're paid to do that work. You should also have someone specifically appointed to do your work, not just anyone who's available. This secretary has to understand that you have the right to give him or her work and that he or she is responsible for doing the work properly.
- Never be seen with a steno pad (especially at meetings; you'll be asked to take notes).
- When you start your new job, don't have your boss's secretary introduce you to other staff. Ask him or her to do it. Otherwise you will start off on the wrong foot. The rest of the employees might believe you're part of the support staff.
- Ask your secretary to make sure you're put on circulation lists for departmental information that's necessary for making decisions. It's amazing how seldom women get on these circulation lists (no matter what their rank). This severely limits their knowledge of what's going on in other departments.
- If you're not sure about something, ask a peer (preferably male) to explain it to you. Being too proud to admit you don't know something will not make you successful.
- Decorate your office the same way men do — order the same expensive paintings and plants. Don't bring plants from home — have your company supply them.
- Make sure your furniture is of the same quality as that in the men's offices.
- Watch that your office doesn't take on a cluttered look. Get into the habit of clearing your desk at night.

– Order a briefcase. Don't assume you have to supply your own. *The* status symbol used to be a briefcase; now it appears to be having your own personal computer in your briefcase.

– Order your business cards as soon as you're appointed to the position. The "position" gets the cards, not the person. The person in charge of ordering cards may not come to you, so you may have to take the initiative. Don't have your home phone number on your cards unless it's absolutely necessary.

– Join professional organizations that can put you in touch with your peer groups in different companies.

– Volunteer for things *only if it will help you up the corporate ladder* — for instance, to give you more exposure to higher-ups in the company.

– Never eat at your desk or in the company cafeteria if your peer group eats elsewhere.

– Company-paid subscriptions to magazines are status symbols — order applicable ones that will help you do your job.

– Don't become friends with a male "misfit." This is sometimes done by women who find they don't fit in with any set group, neither the clerical group below them, nor their male peer group members, nor their superiors. There seems to be one male misfit in every office. This man isn't accepted by his peers for some reason. However, he's very acceptable to the new woman manager, who thinks, "At least one of my peers has accepted me." Men like this often make a beeline for such women out of loneliness. The chances are he's a misfit because *he* doesn't know the rules himself!

– Attend only those meetings that will be of use to you. Send your secretary to take notes for you at unimportant meetings. If you attend, be on time!

– If asked to take minutes at a management meeting, bring your secretary to do so, explaining that you can't participate properly when taking notes for others.

– Accept only positions that will teach you something. If you feel you can adequately perform all the duties of a new position, you're overqualified already. Ask yourself this question every time you accept a new position, be it a promotion in the same company or one with a new company.

– Ensure that you receive the same training and educational opportunities as your peer group. Watch for and be open for any on-the-job or off-site training allowed by your company. Those in management positions usually have many opportunities to obtain further development. Investigate and find out what's available.

– Most people who are fired or forced to quit do so not because of incompetence but because of personal conflicts or office politics. Be wary of this.
– Don't allow yourself to be the office scapegoat. Use your assertiveness training. Don't put yourself down.
– Learn to be a good "team player." Quit playing solitaire.
– Don't act alone. Enlist allies, especially when dealing with controversial issues.
– Don't attempt to hold back vital information merely for your own benefit.
– Assess your co-workers' strengths and weaknesses, then try to avoid rubbing their noses in the latter. Use their strengths to your and their best advantage.
– Know your position duties and do them well. Read your job description and ask your supervisor questions to learn what he or she expects from you.
– If you resign from a position, never burn your bridges and "bad mouth" your former company, boss or co-workers. You never know — ten years down the line when there's been a full turnover of staff, just the right job with the company might open up; but you won't be considered if they check your personnel file and find "sour grapes."
– At management meetings, when everyone's eyes rivet on you at coffee break, implying that they expect you to get the coffee, take charge of the situation by saying, "I take cream and sugar."
– Learn to control such emotions as anger and fear. Men have trouble respecting "emotional" females. Don't cry — it can be really damaging. Try not to lose your cool, no matter what. To avoid the sort of frustrating situation that might trigger an overly emotional response (including the impulse to cry) try to rehearse anticipated bad encounters in advance. As well, remember that all unsatisfactory situations don't have to be dealt with right away. In many cases you can avoid confrontation for the present, give yourself a chance to cool off, and return to the fray when you've worked out a new strategy.

- Be willing to express your ideas to your boss, but never criticize or challenge your boss in public. This is a definite no-no. Even if you think your boss is the dumbest, most poorly organized, most devious person on this earth, don't ever tell anybody. Keep your opinions to yourself. Remember what your mother used to say: "If you can't say something nice, say nothing." (Sometimes your silence tells it all.)
- Remember Rule 14 of the games played in business: never date a co-worker or a client you deal with on a regular basis. You've probably seen what happens to women who do this. If the male is in a higher position, the woman is the one most likely to have to leave when the relationship breaks up. Don't allow yourself to fall into this trap. Stay clear of anything other than platonic relationships with male co-workers and clients.
- Don't be upset if one of your duties is given to someone else. This will allow you to go on to bigger and better things.
- Learn the proper way to accept compliments on a job well done.
- If your boss is weak and indecisive, ask for written guidelines relating to areas in which you do or do not have the authority to make decisions. Explain that this is to ensure that she or he (the boss) isn't "bothered" with trivial details. Not only will you be making more decisions, but your boss may be glad to toss them to you. This decision making can then be listed on your job description and later on your résumé.
- Don't talk about your highest personal ambitions (especially to male peers). Discuss only your next promotional goal. This advice may seem a little ambiguous since I also advised you to let your supervisor know where you want to go. In this case, I mean co-workers, not bosses and personnel-department staff. Your co-workers are likely to say, "Who does she think she is? She says she's hoping to be the manager of this department eventually. If she thinks she's going to be my boss some day, she's got another think coming." Then they'll do everything they can to sabotage your efforts. Choose carefully whom you tell about your ambitions, especially if you're the only woman in an otherwise all-male environment. It's still difficult for many men to see themselves reporting to a woman. In fact, it scares the hell out of them!
- Whatever your boss thinks is important, make it important to you

too. You should certainly express your ideas about how something should be done, but if he or she likes a job done a certain way — do it that way. Never dismiss your boss's priorities as unimportant.

- Your boss's time is important. Do anything you can to make his or her job run more smoothly, but don't hover and get in the way. Be organized and try to anticipate questions your boss may need answered.

- Act impeccably. Perform every act as if it were the only thing in the world that mattered.

- Have a sense of urgency about what you're doing. Don't dawdle and put in time.

- Never reveal all of yourself to other people at work. Hold something in reserve, so that people are never quite sure if they really know you. If you think about it, how much do you know about the private life of your boss?

- Plan your time. Think of time as a friend, not an enemy. Don't waste it doing things that are unimportant.

- Accept your mistakes and learn from them. Don't repeat mistakes, but don't try to be a perfectionist at everything, either.

- Don't go after power only for your own personal good. Aim instead to help others along the way. You'll benefit in the end.

- Don't complain to your supervisor about the behaviour of your peers unless what they are or aren't doing directly affects how you do your job.

- Develop your own informal lines of communication to learn what's happening in other departments of your company.

- Know how your company deals with expense accounts (and don't always go bargain-express.) Use your expense account wisely. Women seem to register at the cheapest hotels they can find and order the cheapest meals they can buy. Don't do this to yourself. Believe me it won't earn you any points, and you'll be labelled as "cheap." But don't go to the other extreme of using the most expensive hotels and restaurants. There's got to be a happy medium. Find out what others in your peer group do when they travel. Follow their lead.

- Have your secretary make travel arrangements for you. Don't feel you have to do it yourself.

TIPS FOR FEMALE TRAVELLERS

If your company doesn't provide a travel agent, get one yourself. Many women still go directly to the airline to buy tickets, but often miss out on special offers from other airlines, or spend hours on the phone determining this themselves. Have your secretary phone for you. My travel agent not only finds the best airline tickets, hotel accommodations and car rentals, but will deliver the tickets to my door if I wish.

Numerous surveys have shown that travel-industry service personnel don't always know how to treat the woman business traveller.

Do you travel on business? If so, these tips may help you have a safer, less hectic trip.

– When travelling out of the country make sure you have additional medical coverage.
– Know your blood type in case of emergency.
– Put identification *inside* your bag as well as outside, in case your luggage tag is lost.
– Pack nylons, belts and other small items inside shoes.
– Select appropriate luggage. Make sure at least one bag is a carry-on size. Don't pack as if you're going on vacation. Just pack one or two outfits suitable for the trip. Try to pack uncreasable outfits. If you find that they're creased when you unpack, ask the hotel to send up an ironing board and iron. If this isn't possible, try hanging them in the bathroom when you shower, or try brushing your curling iron over the clothes. (It worked for me in a pinch!)
– Keep important documents, traveller's cheques and jewellery on your person or in a carry-on bag, purse or briefcase. This might also include a few basic survival items — panty hose, a toilet kit, a change of underwear, etc., in case your bags don't arrive when you do. I learned this lesson on a trip I made to Maui, Hawaii, to conduct seminars. It took my bags twenty-six hours to come from Oahu to Maui. I had so much carry-on luggage (my leader's guides and films), that I didn't have room to carry a "survival kit." Thank goodness the clothes arrived before I had to start instructing or I would have had to purchase a complete outfit (I had travelled in slacks).

- Allow plenty of time for connecting flights. You might be able to make connections in twenty minutes, but your luggage isn't likely to (especially if you're changing planes). It may be best to retrieve your bags and book them forward as you go.
- Always check for damage on a rental car, and make sure it's noted on the contract.
- Check to see if your own car-insurance company offers car-rental insurance. Taking extra car insurance from rental firms is very expensive and unnecessary if you can get it through your own insurance agency.
- Book into hotels that are advertised as "business" hotels rather than "tourist" hotels. You're less likely to get screaming children running up and down the hallways.
- Make sure your hotel reservation is guaranteed with a payment or credit-card number for the first night. (A confirmed reservation that is not guaranteed will only hold your room until 6:00 p.m.)
- When checking in, let the hotel know you're there on business. Give them your business card. Most hotels have corporate rates.
- Don't rely solely on the hotel's wake-up call. Carry a small alarm clock of your own as backup.
- Some hotels now provide small safes in their hotel rooms. There is normally a daily fee for their use. If a room safe is not available, leave valuables in the hotel safe (seldom necessary on business trips).
- Plan on doing something at night. You should explore the place you're visiting, not just stay in the hotel. See the sights, go to the theatre, or go to an interesting restaurant. If you're not sure what's happening, ask at the hotel's front desk.
- When you travel with male colleagues, don't meet in your hotel room or invite people for a drink in your room. This eliminates the problem of guests that overstay their welcome and reduces the risk of having to cope with unwanted advances.
- When the only place you have for a business meeting is your room, ask the hotel to arrange a suite for you. I've had business meetings in rooms that had a table and chairs set up for a business meeting. The room had a hide-a-bed so the bed was out of sight.

- If your room doesn't appear suitable for a meeting, try a quiet corner of a restaurant.
- Don't feel that you should eat only in your room if you're alone. Have a leisurely meal in the dining room and enjoy yourself!
- When dining, expect a decent table where you have some privacy. Do not accept a table next to a swinging kitchen door! (This is my pet peeve, and I quickly ask for a more suitable table.)
- Your bartender or server should not pass a note to you or serve you an unrequested drink without discussing the situation with you first. If you wish to be alone, tell the bartender.
- You deserve respect. If you're addressed as "sweetie" or "honey" by hotel or restaurant employees, discuss it with the manager.
- If you're entertaining guests at a restaurant, make it clear to the server (or when you're making the reservation) that the bill is to be charged to your room. It's hard for waiters and waitresses to know whom to bill if there are three or four people at the table. Make their job easier.
- It is customary to tip fifteen percent, but if you're uncertain about the hotel's tipping policies, ask the manager.
- If there are too many things that go "bump" in the night, turn up the air conditioner — the steady hum of the fan will muffle many of the noises. If you have noisy neighbours, complain to the front desk. If you are not satisfied with how they handle this, complain directly to the manager.
- Take pity on the hotel staff. When you've asked room service to bring a meal, a travelling iron, etc., to your room, don't answer the door while improperly dressed (a chronic complaint of room-service staff).
- If a late check-out is required, notify the front desk. The bellhop can keep your luggage in a storage room.

Safety tips
- Use your business card on your luggage tags. That way, if you're leaving the city, thieves won't be able to tell from looking at your luggage where your (now unoccupied) home is.
- When you register at a hotel, the clerk may announce the number of your room and give you directions on how to find it so others

in the lobby can overhear the information. If this happens, tell the clerk you'd like another room and explain why. Hotels ought to take care to avoid this practice, which can put a woman in jeopardy. If women complain every time hotels make this mistake, the staff will learn not to do it.

– Have a bellhop check your room for security. If your room has a balcony, the doors should be secured.

– *When you're settled in your room, determine where the fire escapes are (identify at least two outlets, so you have alternatives). Count the number of rooms from your suite to the fire escapes, and whether they are to the left or right of your room.* (If a fire were to occur, you might not be able to see the exit and might have to crawl along the floor and count rooms to get there.) *Open the exit door to make sure it isn't locked. Determine whether it's an outside escape or part of the building itself.* Look out your room window to notice the height of your room and the nature of your surroundings. Notice whether and how windows open: do they slide right to left, left to right, straight up, what?

– *When you retire at night, place your room key on the bedside table within easy reach. If a fire should occur, take the key with you when you leave the room.* You may have to return to your room if the smoke is too heavy, or if the fire is too close to your room. If you don't have your key, you may be stranded in a hallway that's an inferno.

– *Never use an elevator if there's a fire.* The elevators will automatically go to the floor where the fire is situated and will not leave that floor because the buttons are often heat-sensitive (to respond when someone has a finger on the button).

– After your room is made up, hang the "Do Not Disturb" sign on the door (even when you're not there) to discourage thieves.

– If you're arriving late at night, call your hotel and let them know you're on your way. Many have an airport pickup service.

– In a strange city, take a cab when going out after dark. This eliminates having to walk from a dark parking lot.

Some hotels now provide both non-smoking floors and "women traveller's" rooms. These rooms provide such welcome amenities as:

   – skirt hangers (missing in far too many hotels)

- packages of nail-polish remover (it's against airline regulations to carry bottles of inflammable substances on airplanes)
- hand and body lotion
- shampoo and cream rinse
- a shower cap
- a sewing kit
- soap for hand laundry
- shoe polish
- a make-up mirror
- a woman's disposable razor
- a full-length mirror
- full-power plugs near the vanity for hair dryers and curling irons. (I can remember being forced to kneel on the floor of my hotel room using the television as a mirror so I could use the only full-power plug in my room.)

When booking a room, have your secretary ask specifically for a "woman traveller's" room. Hotels that don't offer this amenity will learn to do so if enough women ask for it. Statistics indicate that already more than thirty percent of business travellers are women (this percentage is increasing steadily as women move into higher positions), and hotels are learning to cater to their needs.

CHAPTER THIRTEEN

NETWORKING, MENTORS AND AFFIRMATIVE ACTION

NETWORKING

Networking is the practice of making and using contacts. This is a continual process that goes on in the work world as well as the social circuit. It can be done at seminars, conventions, professional meetings or the neighbourhood community club. (Friends and acquaintances form a large network that may seldom be used in a business sense.) Many professional organizations encourage members to get together to exchange leads. For example, if a new company has moved into town, there will probably be a need for office furniture, office supplies, recruitment of staff, etc., and network contacts can keep you informed so you can follow up and offer your product or service.

Watch how men network. In professional and business groups, business cards are exchanged with an ease that surprises some women. To most women, this appears to be a "hard sell" of the individual, and they're reluctant to pass out their cards to just anyone. Men use networking to help each other, and the contacts they make in this business-card exchange make it possible. When a man needs a particular kind of expertise, he'll look through his business cards, put a name to a face, remember the impression that person made on him (possibly from notes put on the back of the business card), and phone the person to set up a meeting.

If you're a true networker, when you enter a room full of people you will spend a few seconds deciding whether you should pursue a conversation or move on to another group. If you meet an interesting prospect, you will spend a few minutes getting acquainted and exchanging business cards. Then you might make notes on the back of the card explaining what this person can do for you, or what you can do for them. You then follow up at a later date.

Rifling through the phone book and making cold calls is now outdated. Networking is far more fun and less threatening. At a networking function, you don't have to pay for a potential client's lunch; he's or she's there already waiting for your information.

Most women don't network nearly as well as men. Unfortunately, some don't even have business cards! If your company won't give you business cards, get some made for yourself.

When women need help, instead of looking elsewhere they should look through their collection of business cards, or check the membership roster of organizations they belong to. They'll probably find the specialist they require listed there. That's what networking is all about. It's people helping people.

If I contact a specialist for advice, it doesn't necessarily mean that the only person I will help in return is that particular person. Others may call on me for help, and pass their particular expertise on to someone else. Eventually, the circle will get back to me with someone helping me (with no obligation in return).

Networkers believe that every new person might be an opportunity to identify a new client or reach new markets. When approaching a new person, start your networking by asking the person what they do. This is the best icebreaker of all. People like to talk about their product or service. They in turn will do the same to you, and the networking process is on its way.

As a female underling within a company, when you see that a woman has been promoted in your company, send her a congratulatory letter. Later ask her for lunch (you pay) and discuss what steps she took to get to the position she's in now. You can also ask her advice regarding your progress in the company and what she would suggest you do to get ahead. This lunch should be initiated about three months after she's had a chance to settle into her position — but send the letter right away.

Anyone who can't network will be left behind, so you owe it to yourself to learn how to do it. Here are some of the essentials for networking:

- Get involved in as many things as you can and make as many contacts as possible. Meeting the right people is the key, so be selective about what groups you join.
- Remember, everyone you meet has the potential to help you in business. This could even include Johnny's teacher, whose husband may be in a business that will need your services.
- Make sure your contacts know what you do. Make up brochures if necessary, or have your business card explain what you do.
- Don't wait for others to introduce you to new people. Step up and do the honors yourself. Being shy will just hold you back.
- Unless someone is a competitor, never withhold information when you see something you can do for someone (even a person who in all probability will never be able to help you in return). Your help will be remembered, and that person could pass on information that may help *you* in the future.
- When you get a possible lead, do something about it immediately. Send a letter, or your brochure, or set up a meeting or luncheon to discuss what you can do for the contact. Don't procrastinate!
- Let people know if there's been any change in what you're doing — such as a new product or service you're offering. Keep up-to-date mailing lists and use them.
- When you have the information you need to evaluate a potential client, make sure you don't waste time on clients that you can't use. Don't give eighty percent of your time for twenty percent of your business. Concentrate on those clients that will keep giving you continued volume business.
- Use your listening skills when networking. Don't allow yourself to overlook important information about potential clients.

Networks step over hierarchical boundaries and give you access to all levels of management within a company. They enable you to go to the actual decision maker directly, without the need to work through the intervening layers of people who can't make the decision. Meeting the decision maker at a conference gives you access to that level ten times more quickly than the traditional route. Mingling with the right group and joining the right organization is a necessity for successful networking, not a luxury, as some companies contend.

As an employee, use your network to help keep your company

ahead of your competitors. Ask your contacts to suggest potential clients to you if they don't themselves need your services or products.

MENTORS

If you talk to successful women, many will tell you that somewhere along the line they had a mentor (at least part-time). A mentor is a strong, powerful person who sees raw talent and helps people expand and utilize their unique skills. They encourage what appear to be ordinary people to achieve success because they see the hidden talent that these individuals possibly didn't realize they had. The mentor provides information and moral support to help them through good and bad times.

Such a person may be an influential senior officer of the employee's company, possibly approaching retirement, but definitely on the lookout to build the company by developing talent among younger employees. It could be a friend of your parents; or a best friend who knows the right people. A mentor is anyone who guides you and keeps you from getting into trouble as you progress up the ladder. This person will stop you from making mistakes that even your male peers make; this will allow you to skip rungs in your promotional climb.

Have you been lucky enough to find a mentor? I've had two in my life. My first mentor was very helpful to me. He was Jim Cebuliak, the president and owner of the Territorial Group of Companies. I admired him because, with little formal training, he had taken a small company and in a short time expanded it into a multi-company empire. I first met him in my job interview and was subsequently hired to head the human resources department for his companies. He needed to have up-to-date personnel system implemented right away, was in on everything I did, and was very supportive of what I was doing.

Understandably, some of the senior executives balked at the extra work the implementation of these new procedures caused them. Some had little formal college or university training and objected to the "newfangled" systems that were being put in place. I reported directly to Jim, so if the managers objected to anything I was doing, they had to complain to him, not me.

He also helped me deal with the more difficult managers and

department heads. I learned more about handling difficult people from him than from anyone else in my life. He was highly respected not only by his management staff but by his employees as well.

My second mentor materialized when I needed him. I had more than seven years' experience in human resources, while my boss had only six months. The difficulties of reporting to someone who so clearly lacked the necessary qualifications caused me considerable frustration and, eventually, anger.

One day I was having a meeting with the man who eventually became my mentor regarding the reclassification of several positions in his department. At the end of the session, he asked me if something was bothering me. I hadn't been aware that my frustration was so obvious. He appeared to be the kind of man who could keep a confidence, so I explained what was happening to me. (Also, I was ready to quit because of the situation and felt I had nothing to lose by talking about it.) He listened intently, then suggested that I transfer laterally to another department, stay in that department until I was two positions higher, then apply for a position in my old department (which would have made me my boss's boss!). My boss, who was incompetent, was not likely to be promoted higher than his present position.

This man was trying to be my mentor, but I just didn't know what he was talking about! I didn't understand the games played in business. I couldn't see the wisdom in his advice because I felt I had made human resources my specialty and couldn't see that working in another department would be the way to climb my particular ladder. I blew it, didn't follow his advice, and became so discouraged I left the company.

I didn't understand how wise his counselling was until I started doing research for this book and learned about the games played in business. In retrospect, if I had taken his advice, I would probably be my former boss's boss, and still be working for the organization. As it turned out, shortly after that time I started my own business.

Think back. You've probably had someone who has been a mentor and you may not have recognized it. Was there someone in your past who brought out your talents and abilities and helped you "stretch" your boundaries of knowledge?

As a woman climbing the corporate ladder, I urge you not to forget to seek that "raw talent" in other men and women and obtain the satisfaction of watching them grow. Look for those who have not had the opportunity to use their talents and abilities. Pull them in when you see them headed for trouble. Give constructive criticism, and be the first to praise them when they've done a good job.

Unfortunately, male mentors for women are still a rare breed. Perhaps this is because such a relationship is still likely to attract gossip and speculation that sexual "favours" may be part of the deal. However, if a man is willing to take this chance with his reputation, then the woman has to as well. The pluses far outweigh the minuses unless there are sexual overtones mixed in with the help received. Women should never accept the latter kind of "help" up the ladder. The help they accept must have no strings attached!

Occasionally there is a negative side to having a mentor. The mentor may take on a protégé for the wrong reasons — out of paternal or maternal feelings, or to reinforce his or her own sense of power. Or the protégé may have been looking for a surrogate parent. Often a mentor may dump too many responsibilities and tasks on the protégé, who burns out and rebels, with negative consequences.

I do encourage receiving help from a mentor. But watch that this person doesn't take over your life and make all the decisions for you. Listen to his or her advice, but remember that you should be the judge of whether to take it or not.

Occasionally, as a protégé progresses up the ladder, the mentor may become very critical of everything the protégé does. He or she can't seem to please the mentor no matter what. This can be devastating. Can you guess what's happening? The protégé is getting too close and too good, becoming a threat to the mentor. The mentor reacts by making almost impossible demands.

How should you handle this if it happens to you? For your own survival, you must wean yourself from your mentor. Very likely, you no longer need this kind of help. I knew one woman who almost destroyed her chances for promotion in a company when this happened to her. Her trusted mentor suddenly became very critical, and she believed he was right. As an observer, I was able to see what was happening and saved her many months of self-doubt.

Fortunately, a mentor may remain a loyal and good friend even when the protégé reaches the mentor's level. The protégé can now give the mentor peer support — which can be very valuable indeed.

AFFIRMATIVE ACTION

Do you personally believe that affirmative action is good or bad? Have you benefited from affirmative action? Or are you part of the majority who haven't been affected by it?

There are pros and cons to affirmative action. The pros, of course, are that companies are forced by the government to hire certain types of employees through a quota system. Without this kind of requirement, many companies would still be hiring pre-dominantly white, male, Anglo-Saxons. Affirmative-action pro-grams also give members of underrepresented groups the oppor-tunity to prove their worth.

However, there are drawbacks to such programs. Often a woman who has been appointed to a position under an affirma-tive-action policy finds herself labelled a "token woman." The assumption may be that the "token woman" isn't really qualified for the job — that she's there only because of the "quota system." With that kind of attitude to overcome, many women feel they have to prove that they're not only as good as but better than their male peers. Of course, some of them fail, and the prejudices are reinforced.

Canada's federal affirmative action program is mandatory within the federal government. Compliance with certain affirma-tive-action provisions is also required for contractors doing busi-ness with the Canadian federal government. As well, the govern-ment encourages voluntary affirmative action in private-sector firms. (There is little doubt, however, that voluntary programs do not work.)

Today, many of Canada's sixty-seven chartered banks have equal-opportunity programs in place. The rest are gearing up to comply with federal regulations. The Royal Bank has annual per-formance reviews to identify potential fast-trackers of both sexes, plus employer-sponsored training — either within the bank or at a university — to give even high-school graduates the credentials they need to advance.

American affirmative action (or equal-opportunity) legislation requires employers to hire a certain percentage of workers from minority groups.

There are no easy answers to this problem. Only time will tell whether affirmative action has worked for women as a group.

CHAPTER FOURTEEN

COULD I BE A SUCCESSFUL ENTREPRENEUR?

"I have my own business!" Who hasn't wished at one time or other that this statement were true? It's a magic phrase that motivates and challenges many, becomes reality for some, but remains only a dream for most.

Until I re-entered the work force, learned the necessary business practices, and gained the self-confidence to go after the carrot — owning my own business — I felt as if I was wasting away. Working for others often left me unsatisfied; I always seemed to "have the brakes on."

However, since I opened my own business in May 1982, life has truly begun for me. No more having to do things I felt were unnecessary or redundant. No more red tape. Each and every hour I spend working for my business has a direct bearing on whether my company makes it or not. The person who benefits most from my work is myself. I am not working so someone else can reap most of the profit. As a result, my energy level is greater. I waste less time and put every minute towards productive work. Mind you, I miss the perquisites — the coffee and lunch breaks, the paid holidays, and the functions, training opportunities and other frills that large companies offer. I'm also working for the hardest boss I'll ever work for, because my expectations for myself are higher than those most bosses would set.

As the following tables show, the number of women in Canada who have taken the plunge into self-employment and/or owning their own business has increased considerably since the 1970s.

Table 14:1
Self-Employed in Canada

Source: Statistics Canada's Labour Force Survey ('000)

	1978	1979	1980	1981	1982	1983	1984	1985	1986
Total both sexes	1193	1251	1310	1352	1380	1440	1480	1549	1556
Male (all ages)	923	958	990	1029	1039	1071	1080	1118	1141
% of self-employed	77.4	76.6	75.6	76.1	75.3	74.4	73.0	72.2	73.3
15 to 24	69	71	66	69	72	75	77	72	66
25+	854	887	925	960	967	996	1003	1046	1075
Female (all ages)	270	293	320	323	341	369	400	431	415
% of self-employed	22.6	23.4	24.4	23.9	24.7	25.6	27.0	27.8	26.7
15 to 24	61	71	72	58	66	73	73	78	69
25+	210	223	248	265	275	296	327	353	346

Table 14:2
Women Small-Business Owners as a Percentage of all Proprietors Canada, 1970-1982

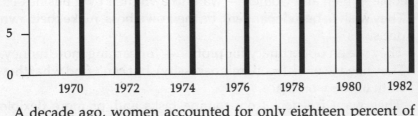

A decade ago, women accounted for only eighteen percent of small businesses. Right now, in the United States, five times as many women as men are starting small businesses, and Canada isn't far behind, with three times as many women as men doing so. In Canada, twice as many women are succeeding. Within the next two years, it's predicted, women will own half the small businesses in the U.S. and Canada!

The sharp increase is largely because of the changing economy and the growing number of women entering the labour market. Women are finding different work in a market in which technology has eliminated many clerical and service positions. As well, women's greater need for flexible working conditions and their tendency to become impatient with the rules of men's business games have encouraged them to look for situations in which they can make their own rules.

INCENTIVES AND DISINCENTIVES TO SELF-EMPLOYMENT

What motivates most people to become self-employed? Some have been turned off being someone else's employee by their lack of opportunity to walk through the doors of management. Statistics show that the majority of them were out of work, felt rejected by their existing employers, or felt insecure about their future with their present company. They were attracted to the idea of owning their own business by the independence they thought they would have. They perceived that there would be more rewards for outstanding performance, and that they would be able to go at their own high-energy pace without having to worry about stepping on anyone's toes or intimidating their colleagues and superiors. Some saw a market that wasn't being serviced. Others came into a sum of money that gave them the opportunity of at least contemplating the idea of being self-employed. Many were just drawn in by the romance of it all.

The following list identifies the most common reasons why people — men and women — want to own their own businesses.
– They wish to be independent, be their own boss, make their own decisions.
– They see an opportunity for profits — for earning more money.
– They need to work (economic necessity), but can't find what they want in the workplace.
– They want freedom from routine tasks and/or more flexible hours; or they need to stay at home with their families.
– They're looking for personal satisfaction.
– They've identified a market that is not being served.

Of course, there are problems to be faced if you decide to go it alone (especially if you're contemplating running a cottage-industry business out of your home). Lack of security is a major one. What would happen if you became ill? (Disability insurance bought in advance can help with this one. If there is a professional group you can join, you may be able to get a group rate on premiums, which can be very costly otherwise.) Can you obtain the necessary financing? What happens if your company goes broke? How about the loneliness you might feel if you work alone out of your home? Possibly you'll miss the companionship of co-workers at coffee and lunch breaks? How about the missed Christmas parties and company barbecues? Will you be able to work with your children underfoot? These are all possible negatives.

THE SUCCESSFUL ENTREPRENEUR

Suppose you've decided the advantages outweigh the disadvantages? Does that mean you're ready to take the plunge? Not quite. First you should ask yourself if you've properly assessed your chances of success. Do you have what it takes to launch a business on your own and make it fly? Ask yourself if you have the characteristics of a successful entrepreneur. The successful entrepreneur usually:

– is a good risk taker, not afraid of failure;
– is not content to be someone's employee (likes recognition, dislikes hierarchies and reporting to a boss, dislikes having to justify all new ideas to others before taking action, etc.);
– is more qualified than those he/she reports to;
– approaches work with as much zest as if it were play;
– is competitive — and expects to win;
– is good at seeing needs that aren't being met and turning them into business opportunities;
– is a positive thinker;
– becomes bored when not challenged;
– likes starting businesses more than running them (a true entrepreneur);
– has good organizational abilities;
– is flexible and open to new ideas;
– has a consistently high energy level;
– is reluctant to seek outside help (less true of women);
– has faith in his or her instincts (or gut reactions);
– can improvise — does not need to do things "by the book";
– judges people by their achievements and abilities rather than their education or pedigree;
– is an avid attender of seminars.

Natural entrepreneurs want to call their own shots, love to wheel and deal, and don't worry about working around the clock if necessary. They have also:

– investigated the need for their product or service;
– evaluated their own preparedness;
– acquired a basic understanding of the business they're entering;
– developed a business plan based on market studies.

True entrepreneurs aren't content to leave things as they are. They have confidence in their own ideas and are willing to accept the hard work and long hours necessary to make a success of their venture.

THE WOMAN ENTREPRENEUR

Studies in the U.S. and Canada comparing the personal characteristics of men and women entrepreneurs have found that women entrepreneurs:

– are younger than their male counterparts, usually under 39 (men are usually over 50);
– have several years more education than men entrepreneurs;
– are significantly less optimistic and less impulsive than their male counterparts;
– are more willing than men to admit when they don't know something;
– are more inclined than men to use written communication and to read business publications and books;
– spend anywhere from six to ten months studying the feasibility of a business before committing themselves.
– start companies that are less profitable in the long run than those started by men because the companies are mainly in the service industry. The big money is in manufacturing and the production of goods, but it's also much riskier financially.

According to a study conducted by Robert D. Hisrich of Boston College and Candida Brush of H and P Associates, the typical woman entrepreneur "is the first born; from at least a middle-class family; has a college degree with a liberal-arts major; is married with children, has a spouse who is supportive and in a professional or technical occupation." She usually works in a "traditional women-business area (retail, consulting, personal services); [and] started business because of lack of interest in [available job] areas and job frustration." Her business is usually young and small, with revenues of less than $500,000; and she maintains a controlling interest in the firm.

STRENGTHS OF WOMEN ENTREPRENEURS

Women business owners may appear overly cautious and prudent in their expenditures, but it's their saving grace. They pay themselves realistic salaries and have lower expectations of returns than men. They keep their debt load much lower. It's been determined that this quality more than any other is the reason women succeed so well in business — they don't overextend their credit and get in over their heads financially!

Another advantage some women entrepreneurs have is their ability to type and use word processors. Male entrepreneurs often have to hire people to do secretarial and clerical work (or they conscript their wives to do it). Women are less averse to tackling anything that needs doing. They're not too proud to clean out the employees' washroom or vacuum the office when necessary. Men seldom feel comfortable stooping to this level of work.

Many women work out of their homes, which also helps keep overhead low. In my case, several of my competitors went out of business just as I was starting up. The reason they failed appears to be that their overhead was too high. I conduct my business out of my home instead of renting an office. I do my own typing, and I rent training facilities only as I need them.

Most women are great at bartering, too. (For example, I have offered seminars in exchange for graphic design work. I get great graphics for one of my brochures, and the graphic artist gets educated.)

Women entrepreneurs have the best chance of profiting from a changing economy. Forty-eight percent of new ventures owned by women offer services or information. Twenty-five percent are in the retail sector, and only five percent fall in the manufacturing sector. Forty-seven percent of women who start their own businesses make it through the first tough years. Male entrepreneurs have a harder time: only twenty-five percent make it through the first three years — mainly because of a too-large debt load and going too big too soon.

Women in business are headed in the right direction by offering goods and services to the small but growing markets of working women and two-income families. They ignore the traditional middle-income mass market targeted by larger corporations. They're also good at defining client needs. If they run into roadblocks in obtaining a product or service they feel *should* be available, instead of looking at it as just another frustration they see it as an opportunity to provide something for themselves and others.

WEAKNESSES OF WOMEN ENTREPRENEURS

The major problems women entrepreneurs have are in finance, marketing and organizational planning. Finance is the most serious of these.

A survey conducted in 1985 by B.C. Women's Programs and the Central Statistics Bureau of the B.C. Ministry of Industry and Small Business Development identified the problems encountered by women business owners at the start up of their businesses as follows:

> The one single problem most frequently encountered by women business owners at the start up of their businesses was difficulty in accessing financing. Over one-third of the women surveyed cited this problem. Almost one-third of the women business owners identified a variety of problems that cannot be easily categorized including time management, financial uncertainty, personnel management, and establishing credibility. The lack of information/training was identified as a barrier by over 9% of the business owners, while almost 11% of the respondents did not experience any major problems when they were establishing their businesses.

Women also identified the unpredictability of the market, the lack of good part-time, occasional child care, and problems with morale and self-esteem as difficulties for women business owners in particular. The following table ranks the needs of women entrepreneurs.

Table 14:3
Unmet Needs of Business Women

Unmet Need	% of women who perceive the need as a problem
Difficulties obtaining capital	60.5
Lack of appropriate business information	34.2
Lack of encouragement from family and peers	26.9
Shortage of skilled labour	12.3
Shortage of raw materials	6.4

Source: Central Statistics Bureau, Ministry of Industry and Small Business Development, British Columbia

As Table 14:4 shows, it's not always necessary for entrepreneurs to have a high level of education.

Table 14:4
Highest Level of Education Attained
by Women Business Owners

Level	Percent
Non-high school graduate	15.6
High school graduate	20.1
Incomplete college or university	25.3
College diploma/certificate or university degree	26.8
Post-graduate university degree	12.2

Source: Central Statistics Bureau, Ministry of Industry and Small Business Development, British Columbia

TYPES OF SELF-EMPLOYMENT

Suppose you're still undaunted by the drawbacks of self-employment. What kind of business could you start?

Part-Time Business

Many self-employed women earn all or a portion of their income by selling door-to-door, or by holding home parties. They sell anything from make-up, to home cleaners, to housewares. The main attraction of this kind of work is its flexibility. Selling time can be arranged around the needs of the family, and the time-wasting commute to and from work is eliminated. There are very few prerequisites, so even those with minimal education can make a go of it. The main requirement for this kind of career is strong motivation and selling ability.

A major disadvantage is that people involved in this kind of work don't receive a regular salary or any company benefits. Another disadvantage for some is that it can be difficult to concentrate with little children underfoot. Women seem to survive this, though; as one woman said to me: "I'm so used to doing everything all at once anyway, I know I can handle it!"

It's important to choose the right product or service to sell. (Some women manufacture the products they market. One woman I know of makes custom-made baby quilts for baby showers, flea markets, craft shows, hospital gift shops and small novelty shops. She can't keep up with the demand. She has the advantage of working out of her home doing something she enjoys, and she is well paid for it! Another woman knits custom-made socks for people who have leg casts and need one huge sock to go over their bare toes. She sells her wares in hospital gift shops and does a booming business.)

To be able to sell your product or service properly, you must personally believe that it is better than that of your competitors. Investigate such things as the profit margin, how much you have to invest initially, and your anticipated return on investment. How much inventory will you have to keep on hand, and can you afford the investment and the financial obligations it might impose? Will you need a car to deliver your product? What will your car expenses be? How about child care? Will the job pay you enough to reward you for what you put into it?

Although profits may be small initially, you may be able to benefit from tax deductions. For instance, if you use one room in your home to store inventory or conduct business, a portion of mortgage payments or rent can be deducted as a business expense, as can part of your home utility and telephone bills. You can deduct the cost of equipment and other capital expenditures, advertising costs and sometimes even your baby-sitter's salary. If you use your car, your out-of-pocket expenses can be deducted. (However, the new tightened Revenue Canada tax laws will make it difficult to claim business expenses unless you can prove that there really is a business by pointing to such things as your business phone, filing cabinets, desks, computers, storage facilities for inventory, etc.)

Professional Stay-at-homes
Many professional women spend a portion of their day or week working in a formal office setting and the rest of the time working at home. One female lawyer had her company install a computer terminal in her house so she could prepare legal briefs for court in the comfort and quiet of her home (her children were of school age).

The computer age has changed things for many people in such professions as engineering, consulting, software distributing and writing. Secretaries, too, can benefit from this. One woman worked for an engineer and dealt with specifications that were often done in draft form first, then updated and changed several times before final submission. Many of these "specs" took most of a day to prepare. She obtained permission to have a terminal in her home and was able to work there while doing long-term assignments. She did the company's accounting at home as well. Her only office appearances were to pick up and deliver assignments and supplies.

Companies that really don't need employees to work in an office setting are realizing the advantages of having them work at home. Employers save money because they don't have to provide office space and the administrative overhead that goes with it. If you think your company can benefit from this kind of arrangement, suggest that they try it. Outline the savings they will make if they don't need to supply you with an office. Possibly all you have to do is come in once a week or so to pick up your next batch of work and to drop off completed assignments.

For a home-based worker using a computer, the company will incur the initial expense of hooking up the computer, but from then on it will save money. Some employers balk at this idea because they believe home-based workers' productivity will suffer if there's no one around to oversee them. It's true that workers who succeed at working out of their homes tend to be highly independent and have minimal needs for social contacts while working. In fact, such people seem to produce *more* at home, partly because of the lack of interruptions.

If you can choose this route, it's advisable to set up a real office and make sure family members know you're not to be disturbed when working — unless there's an earthquake.

Franchises
Another kind of business worth investigating is a franchise. In this case, the parent company supplies guidelines — you're not out there on your own. It is a great testing and learning ground for wary entrepreneurs.

STARTING YOUR OWN BUSINESS
If you're thinking of starting a business you'll have to give it plenty of thought. Read everything you can. Do your homework *before* jumping in. Know the rules about licensing and government regulations.

You'll have to decide whether to be a sole proprietor, go into partnership, or incorporate. These are important decisions, and you should find out what each type of company involves before choosing one. Starting a business with a partner could be compared to getting married. Partners must have compatible goals. It helps if they're complementary rather than identical in personality, skills and abilities. You and your partner must decide *before* starting your business what might go wrong, and work out potential solutions in advance.

TEN STEPS TO A SUCCESSFUL BUSINESS

1. Get a marketable idea.
2. Know your product.
3. Get the professional help you need (lawyer, accountant, advice from federal business development agency).
4. Organize your time and work area.
5. Set *realistic* goals.
6. Know your markets and how to reach them.
7. Research your competition.
8. Don't oversell your service or product.
9. Maintain a professional image.
10. Promote your own business.

KNOW YOUR BUSINESS – AND YOURSELF

Do you know enough about this particular business to run it successfully? As a business owner, you will be expected to understand all aspects of your business: pricing, purchasing, financing, accounting, marketing, etc. It's crucial that you recognize your weaknesses and areas of inexperience and either improve those skills through training or make use of appropriate consultants and advisors.

Being your own boss can offer great personal satisfaction, but with it comes the responsibility for making and living with your decisions. The right decision can bring profit and success; the wrong decision can cost you money. Making too many wrong decisions can put you out of business. Be ready!

Your own character and personality will greatly influence the success of any new business. Here are some things you should ask yourself before you plunge in with both feet:

1. Do you possess the right combination of ambition, determination and self-esteem?

2. Can you cope with the stress of personal and financial risks you'll be taking when you strike out on your own?

3. Are you patient enough to deal with employees, clients and suppliers?

4. How long will you be expected to work — four hours, eight hours, twelve hours a day? Do you have the energy level to meet these needs?

5. How creative are you? Can you identify needs that no one else sees?

6. Are you a self-starter, or do you need someone else to help "get your motor running"?

7. Do you have the time it takes to start a business (ten to twelve hours a day, initially)?

8. If you have family obligations, do you have time to devote to both family and business without feeling guilty?

9. If you're married, will your spouse give you the moral support you need to operate a business?

10. Should you maintain your current employment and work part-time at your business, or should you jump in with both feet right away? I found the first alternative better for me. I offered training and development seminars on weekends and in the evenings years before I started my full-time business.

11. Have you had previous business experience? If not, are you willing to obtain the necessary training, knowledge and skills?

12. Can you and your family survive a financial failure? (The first two years can be dicey.)

13. Are you willing to work *very hard*?

14. Are you able to organize your time and that of others you may be called upon to supervise?

15. Do you understand how to lead, motivate and discipline employees? Do you know how to delegate responsibility?

16. Are you good at keeping records, or will you have to hire a bookkeeper or accountant?

17. Do you procrastinate, or are you able to meet deadlines without problems?

18. Can you make decisions?

19. Are you self-confident?

20. Are you able to persevere?

21. Are you a positive thinker?

22. Do you have a sense of what motivates people to buy?
23. Are you willing to take the risk?

MARKETING

Advance research and preparation is crucial in this area. Is there a market for your product or service? Have you done a market survey to confirm this? Have you chosen a "target market" (the most likely group to buy your product or service)? If you don't know where to start, contact firms that specialize in marketing and have them do the research for you. In the long run, they'll proba- bly do it more cheaply and thoroughly than you can. They'll be able to supply information about such things as:
– who your competitors are;
– whether the market you plan to enter is growing or shrinking;
– the general condition of the industry;
– the results of test marketing using sample groups;
– your best target markets and the names of probable clients;
– how your product or service compares to existing competitive products or services;
– what to charge for your product or service initially, and what you could charge eventually as the product or service becomes better known;
– how to break into an existing market or introduce a new product or service;
– the most appropriate media in which to advertise;
– the comparative merits of different types of packaging;
– the best methods of distribution (wholesale, retail, franchise or direct sales);
– your potential market share;
– possible international markets.

PRICING

Watch that you don't undersell your competition. Most women undervalue their products or services. Initially, to prove credibility, you might give a lower rate for a service, but eventually you should raise your price to meet that of your competitors. It's ironic, but if you ask a low price, the consumer expects a low-grade product. On the other hand, if you ask a premium price for your product, the consumer expects a premium product. If your cost is high, you had better offer a high-quality product.

DISTRIBUTION

If you can't get a supplier to carry your product, distribute it yourself. The initial costs will be higher, but the control you'll have may be worth it. It may shock you when you see how many intermediaries there are between the point of production and the consumer — and each of these intermediaries is paid a percentage of the retail price. The result is that the initial production price (unit cost) may be only a small fraction of the retail price. If you want to keep your price low you will have to eliminate as many of these "middlemen" as possible.

FINANCING

Earlier, I identified financing as one of the biggest problems for women in business. One particular source of difficulty is that some women do not have an independent credit rating. As a result their spouse's signature is required on all financial documents. If a woman in such a situation insists on having her own financing, she'll probably obtain only one-quarter of the amount that would be given to her husband. Women are fighting this battle, and many are winning. If you don't have your own credit rating (obtained by having credit cards and bank loans in your own name), I encourage you to start building one now. This will eliminate some of the hassles often experienced by women who wish to borrow money, be it for a mortgage or for starting a business.

How much money will you need? This will be determined by your business plan, which we will discuss. Businesses can be started for as little as $500. Or they may require an inventory worth $500,000. The variation is considerable.

When I started my consulting business, I had a low overhead and no inventory. Time was my major investment. I also had a small nest egg, a typewriter, a telephone and lots of energy. I've never had to borrow money at any time. You may be in the same position.

Make sure you're financially sound before launching into business. You can expect to earn little during the first year — maybe you will just keep your head above water. Therefore, you must have a little "capital" put aside so you don't panic when the going gets tough. For the rest of your financing, bankers or private lenders (family and friends) may be used.

Many people put off starting a business because they assume

they will have to pay large sums out of their small earnings to such professionals as lawyers and accountants. Investigate before making this assumption.

There are two major causes of business failure: poor management and too little money. When you first start a business, it makes good sense to accumulate all the free advice and counsel you can. Many government agencies give free advice to those who take the time to ask. I suggest you contact your provincial ministry of industry and trade for this kind of information. And by all means, pick the brains of successful business owners in your community. Join your local chamber of commerce — get involved and ask questions.

Be prepared to take constructive criticism. Often new entrepreneurs have such a strong commitment to a product, idea or service that they're reluctant to hear any negative comments when this input could save them considerable time and money.

BUSINESS PLAN

I mentioned a business plan earlier. This is a written summary of the overall activities of the business. It shows investors that you've looked thoroughly into the viability of your company. Included in a business plan are:
– a detailed description of the product or service;
– an outline of your marketing strategy;
– a description of your production techniques;
– information about types of employees you may need to hire;
– the history and present state of the business and the outlook for the future (especially important when you take over a business previously owned by others).

When properly prepared, this plan becomes the blueprint for financing. It has to be complete, well organized and factual.

A well-written business plan will be one of the most important elements in the presentation to your banker. It also makes you more organized and aware of pitfalls that may trip you up. A well-written business plan will:
– make your business more real to you (by forcing you to study the cost-volume-profit relationship and indicating when sales projections are too optimistic);
– establish break-even points for you to monitor (this will assist you in watching your cash flow and return on investment);

– make you do a complete market survey to establish your potential market and determine your competition;
– keep you aware of potential danger signals such as drops in the volume of sales, too much inventory in stock, too much money going out compared to what's coming in;
– help you identify staffing needs;
– help you manage and present your company in a professional manner.

ORGANIZING

Watch your profitability. This is done by establishing various systems to monitor profits — e.g., bookkeeping, accounting, data-processing, inventory-control systems, etc. Make sure you have adequate insurance coverage, both property and personal.

My company was too small to need a full-time accountant, so I had an accountant set up my books and show me how to make entries. Because I don't have inventory and there are few transactions, it takes me approximately half an hour per month to do my books. At year-end, I have my accountant do my books and prepare my income-tax forms. You may not be able to manage with so little paperwork. It depends on the size and type of business you own.

STAFFING

You'll be faced with the challenge of finding, interviewing and hiring employees. Be careful not to ask illegal questions in an interview. Managing employees means much more than giving orders. After you hire them, you'll have the task of assigning work, training them and developing their talents.

MANAGING

Management involves the maximum utilization of people, money and other resources to achieve the desired result. Poor management is the largest single cause of business failure. Management skills should be tested *before* the business is established.

Through experience, you'll learn to avoid mistakes and anticipate problems, plan alternatives and handle crises more efficiently. If you have no experience in the type of business you want to start, you should work for someone else who is already well established. Pick their brains and learn as much as you can about their business and how they manage it.

No amount of experience will replace your own feelings of self-confidence about your ability to succeed in business.

PUTTING YOUR DREAMS INTO ACTION

Without the belief that your product or service is better in some way than that of your competitors, you probably won't succeed. If you do believe you have something to offer that your competitors don't, you're ready for the next steps.

1. Prepare your marketing strategy and business plan.
2. Get your money together (or arrange your financing).
3. Decide upon your business's legal obligations, such as licensing and government regulations.
4. Obtain any necessary business licenses.
5. Choose the best location.
6. Set up an accounting system.
7. Determine your pricing schedule.
8. Decide on your advertising strategies (including business cards, brochures and letterhead).
9. Hire staff.
10. Prepare for taxes.
11. Open your business!

When you're ready to launch your company, look into giving a press release (free) to your local newspapers. Give them plenty of lead time. If your product or service is unique, try getting on talk shows, especially those that will reach the market you wish to tap. I've found I get a far better response from one television talk-show appearance than from thousands of dollars' worth of newspaper advertising.

An excellent source of information for the female entrepreneur is Moneca Litton's *Women Mean Business – Successful Strategies for Starting Your Own Business* (see the bibliography), which can give you details on how to start a business *in Canada* (most books are written for American entrepreneurs). Going into business always involves some risk. You can reduce that risk by careful research and thoroughly documented (put it all in writing) advance planning.

On the whole, women who become entrepreneurs gain immense satisfaction from what they're doing. The monetary rewards may be less important than the emotional benefits. Some (for the first time they can remember) really feel good about themselves. They have never before felt the kind of "high" that comes from this sense of accomplishment. Others enjoy being in control of their destinies for the first time in their lives.

Conclusion
Here's a final checklist to help highlight for you the key things you should remember when climbing the corporate ladder.
- Make realistic life and career goals for yourself.
- Get the training you need (especially supervisory training), preferably before accepting a new position.
- Don't expect your employer to "look after" you. Pay for necessary training if your employer won't provide it.
- Make sure your employer knows what your career plans are so you're not overlooked for a promotion.
- Get your home life in order by obtaining help with child care and household chores.
- Stop trying to be Superwoman.
- Think twice before turning down overtime, travelling and relocation requests from your employer.
- Don't take time off from work unless you really need it.
- Discuss only business-related matters on company time.
- Be prepared to make decisions and defend your ideas with facts.
- Don't be a quitter when you run into opposition; instead come up with "plan B," and "plan C" if necessary.
- Be willing to help other women in positions of power.
- Ensure that you have an accurate up-to-date job description.
- Ask for regular performance appraisals (preferably ones that evaluate objective rather than subjective things).
- Practise identifying and dealing with the games played in business.
- Be ready to negotiate for the salary you're worth.
- Know how to apply for senior positions.
- Ask for a written job offer.
- Learn to sell yourself in interviews and to handle illegal questions gracefully.
- When overlooked for a promotion, do something about it!
- Don't manipulate others to get your way; act assertively.
- Beware of self-sabotage and practise positive thinking.

- Be willing to take risks.
- Handle male chauvinism, discrimination and sexual harassment in a calm but firm manner.
- Follow suggested office and travel tips.
- Be an effective networker.
- Find a strong mentor.
- Finally, you may decide to "opt" out completely from the games played in business and seriously look into the possibilities of becoming a female entrepreneur. Whatever you choose, plan carefully, then GO FOR IT!

BIBLIOGRAPHY

Armstrong, Pat. *The Double Ghetto — A Working Majority.* Toronto: McClelland and Stewart, 1978.

Baer, Jean. *How to Be an Assertive (Not Aggressive) Woman.* New York: Signet, 1976.

Berne, Eric. *Games People Play.* New York: Ballantine Books, 1964.

Burack, Elmer; Albrecht, Maryann; and Seitler, Helene. *Growing: A Woman's Guide to Career Satisfaction.* Belmont, Calif.: Lifetime Learning, 1980.

Buskirk, Richard, and Mills, Beverly. *Beating Men at Their Own Game: A Woman's Guide to Successful Selling in Industry.* New York: McGraw Hill Paperbacks Ser., 1980.

Chesler, Phyllis, and Goodman, Emily Jane. *Women, Money and Power.* New York: William Morrow, 1976.

Cook, James. *The Start-Up Entrepreneur.* New York: Harper and Row, 1987.

Dowling, Colette. *The Cinderella Complex.* New York: Simon and Schuster, 1981.

Eichenbaum, Luise and Orbach, Susie. *What Do Women Want — Exploding the Myth of Dependency.* New York: Berkley Books, 1983.

Gallese, Liz Roman. *Women Like Us.* New York: Signet, 1985.

Genfan, Herb, and Taetzsch, Lyn. *How to Start Your Own Craft Business.* Watson-Guptill Publications, 1974.

Gilligan, Carol. *In a Different Voice.* Cambridge, Mass.: Harvard University Press, 1982.

Gillis, Phyllis. *Entrepreneurial Mothers.* New York: Rawson, 1983.

Gordon, Dr. Thomas. *Parent Effectiveness Training: The Tested New Way to Raise Responsible Children.* New York: McKay, 1970.

Gornick, Vivian and Moran, Barbara K. *Women in Sexist Society.* New York: Basic Books, 1971.

Harragan, Betty Lehan. *Games Your Mother Never Taught You.* New York: St. Martin's, 1983. (An absolute MUST!)

————. *Knowing the Score: Play-by-Play Directions for Women on the Job.* New York: St. Martin's, 1981.

Jessup, Claudia, and Chipps, Jean. *The Woman's Guide to Starting a Business.* New York: Holt, Rinehart and Winston, 1976.

Kelly, P.C.; Lawyer, K.; and Baumback, C.M. *How to Organize and Operate a Small Business.* Englewood Cliffs, NJ: Prentice-Hall, 1982.

Kiley, Dan. *The Peter Pan Syndrome.* New York: Dodd Mead, 1983.

La Rouche, Janice. *Strategies for Women at Work.* New York: Avon, 1984.

Landau, Suzanne, and Bailey, Geoffrey. *The Landau Strategy — How Working Women Win Top Jobs.* Toronto: Lester and Orpen Dennys, 1980.

Litton, Moneca. *Women Mean Business: Successful Strategies for Starting Your Own Business.* Toronto: Key Porter Books, 1987.

Loden, Marilyn. *Feminine Leadership, or How to Succeed in Business Without Becoming One of the Boys.* New York: Times Books, 1985.

Mancuso, Joseph. *The Small Business Survival Guide: Sources of Help for Entrepreneurs.* Englewood, NJ: Prentice-Hall, 1980.

Martyn, Sean. *How to Start and Run a Successful Mail Order Business.* New York: David McKay, 1969.

Miller, Dr. Jean Baker. *Toward a New Psychology of Women.* Boston: Beacon Press, 1976.

Moran, Peg. *Invest in Yourself: A Woman's Guide to Starting Her Own Business.* Garden City, NY: Doubleday, 1983.

Scollard, Jeanette R. *The Self-Employed Woman.* New York: Simon and Schuster, 1985.

Scott, Robert. *How to Set Up and Operate Your Office at Home.* New York: Scribners, 1985.

Sheehy, Gail. *Passages.* New York: Dutton, 1976.

Stechert, Kathryn. *Sweet Success — How to Understand the Men in Your Business Life and Win with Your Own Rules.* New York: Macmillan, 1986.

Stewart, Nathaniel. *The Effective Woman Manager — Seven Vital Skills to Upward Mobility.* Ann Arbor, Mi.: Books on Demand, _____ .

Winston, Sandra. *The Entrepreneurial Woman.* New York: Newsweek Books, 1979.

INDEX

ACKNOWLEDGEMENTS

The local media's support and involvement were important to the initial research for this book. They were thirsty for this type of controversial topic. Through newspaper articles, television programs and radio talk shows I was able to get my message to those who eventually contributed to my research. There were three distinct target groups I asked to contact me:

1. managers who might reveal why they weren't promoting women;
2. women who felt they were running into barriers to promotion;
3. women who had achieved success and might be willing to explain how they had done it.

The response was overwhelming! I had to throw out many of my outdated ideas about why women were not being promoted or considered for higher-level positions in business. My thanks to one and all who offered their words of wisdom, to those who helped identify special women in Canada, and to the friends and acquaintances who urged me to put my ideas into a book so that all women could have access to my findings.

My heartfelt thanks and unending gratitude go to my parents, Bob (who passed away on April 6, 1987) and Mabel Hastie, without whose help and moral support I would not have accomplished what I have, and to my children, Mike and Michele, for their assistance and patience during the early years of my second career. Special thanks are also extended to Margaret Allen and Patti Connolly, who edited this book, and Faye Wiesenberg of the Alberta Career Development and Employment Branch, who offered career-counselling advice.